HARMONY &
CONTRAST

A Journey through East Asian Art

Jane Wilkinson & Nick Pearce

N·M·S

NATIONAL MUSEUMS OF SCOTLAND

Published by the National Museums of Scotland,
Chambers Street, Edinburgh EH1 1JF

© Trustees of the National Museums of Scotland 1996

British Library Cataloguing in Publication Data
A catalogue record of this book is available from the
British Library

ISBN 0 7007 0461 2

Designed by the Publications Office, National
Museums of Scotland
Printed in Great Britain by Clifford Press Ltd,
Coventry

Acknowledgements
Susan Leiper for her informed editing and welcome
advice, and the illustrations on page 119.
Sir Victor Sassoon Ivories Trust for the illustration on
page 107.
Kondo Takahiro for the illustration on page 64.
Iwao Akiyama for the illustration on page 90.

CONTENTS

PREFACE

As a Hong Kong businessman I am aware that Scots have long been associated with the development of Hong Kong, contributing to its success. I am very happy therefore to acknowledge the links between Scotland and East Asia by supporting a new permanent exhibition, named in honour of my wife, to enable the National Museums of Scotland to make these important collections of East Asian art accessible to the Scottish public and to visitors from elsewhere.

Gordon Wu　胡應湘

FOREWORD

The East Asian collections in the National Museums of Scotland owe their beginnings to objects brought back from China by Scottish visitors in the early nineteenth century. Since then significant collections of objects have been acquired from China and Japan, and a smaller but nonetheless important collection from Korea.

Although some of these objects have always been on display it has never before been possible to show together the full range and variety of the East Asian collections, including many fragile items such as textiles and paintings.

Now, for the first time, the full extent of these collections is accessible for public enjoyment and understanding in a new permanent exhibition, 'The Ivy Wu Gallery, China, Japan and Korea' and in this book. The gallery is arranged thematically within the three distinct cultures of China, Japan and Korea, and the book takes a complementary approach by grouping the collections according to materials, such as silk, lacquer and porcelain.

We are deeply grateful to Gordon Wu for the generous sponsorship which has led to the creation of the gallery and the book and which will encourage greater understanding of East Asian art and culture in Scotland and throughout the world.

Robert Smith
Chairman of the Board of Trustees of the National Museums of Scotland

'Playing in the snow', part of a triptych illustrating The Tale of Genji, *a tenth-century Japanese novel by Murasaki Shikibu. Signed Toyokuni, a pen name of Kunisada, 1854.*

Japanese Fairy Tale Series, No. 9.

The Serpent With Eight Heads.

Told in English.

by B. H. Chamberlain.

PUBLISHED

BY T. HASEGAWA,

JOURNEY TO THE EAST

Silk, lacquer and porcelain: mere mention of these luxury materials conjures up images of an exotic lifestyle in a far-off land. It was precisely these images that were conveyed to the West by the early traders who brought back almost exclusively luxury goods. Such a trader was Marco Polo, who left Venice in 1271 to travel overland to China. He is said to have spent seventeen years travelling in the East, and his account of Cathay, as he called it, paints a romantic picture of life in China and of Khubilai Khan's palace in Beijing. Later, similar accounts were to whet the European appetite for the foreign and exotic. At the same time, these accounts obscured the hardships endured by the traders, both overland and at sea, and ignored the great cultural traditions that lay behind the luxuries exported to the West.

The demand for items such as silks and spices had linked China with the Roman court of Augustus in the first century BC and with the capital of the eastern Roman Empire, Constantinople, from the fourth century AD. Ideally placed at the gateway between Europe and Asia, the rich Byzantine economy was dependent on trade in the luxury goods of the East. Initially the trade route was overland, with Chinese goods travelling westwards along the Silk Route, and Western goods returning eastwards. The quest for new lands and new products, and the increasing knowledge of navigation and mapmaking in the fifteenth and sixteenth centuries encouraged the establishment of trade routes by sea. The romance of sailing and stories of sea monsters and strange exotic ports fuelled the imagination of artists and craftsmen in both East and West. Design motifs travelled back and forth, as did the form of objects copied by one culture from, and often for, another. The Dutch potteries at Delft used Chinese motifs on their imitations of Chinese blue and white Kraak porcelain, and the Chinese made entire dinner services, often painted with copies of Western prints, for export to Europe.

The copying of oriental forms and designs led to the extravagances of chinoiserie in the eighteenth century and of japonaiserie in the nineteenth century. The Chinese-style interiors of the Royal Pavilion, Brighton, the eclectic architectural fantasy built for the Prince Regent in 1823, indicate the British fascination with Chinese exoticism. Likewise, Japanese curios reaching the West reflected the picaresque idea Westerners had of Japan. However, the study of Japanese art and craftsmanship by the architects William Burges and E W Godwin, the painters Whistler and Rossetti, and interior designers such as William Morris led to the Aesthetic Movement of the 1860s and 1870s.

Book cover for the Japanese fairy-tale Urashima. *Published in English in the early twentieth century.*

This was a reaction against the mass-produced, poor quality domestic furnishings resulting from the industrial revolution. Although the interest in Japanese art, as with the interest in Western medieval art, was somewhat romanticized, it resulted in designs influenced by the Japanese concepts of space, harmony and asymmetry.

It was at this time, when Western powers were expanding, that the Museum (now the Royal Museum of Scotland) was founded. Originally the Industrial Museum of Scotland, established in 1854 as part of the museum movement initiated by the Great Exhibition of 1851, it was housed in a new building in Chambers Street by 1861. The newly acquired industrial objects and works of art were combined with the University of Edinburgh's natural history collections and the museum was known as The Museum of Science and Art. One of its aims was to stimulate students of arts and crafts by giving them access to designs from all over the world.

The East Asian collections in the Museum today reflect Scottish interests and activities in East Asia over the last three hundred years. As colonial officials, soldiers, sea captains, doctors, entrepreneurs, explorers or missionaries, Scots have visited first China, then Japan and latterly Korea since the beginning of the eighteenth century. Though

Cosmetic box of the Ming dynasty, China, made in the reign of the Yongle Emperor (1403-24). Detail shows the reign mark on the base.

many returned to Scotland after travelling or working in the East, some settled permanently. The things they acquired, as souvenirs, for scientific enquiry or as part of systematic collecting, give us significant evidence about the collectors, the societies they visited and the peoples among whom they lived.

Curiosity and a thirst for knowledge, associated with economic expansion, had led to greater worldwide exploration and travel. The collections arriving in museums were no longer considered just as curiosities or antiquities but were classified and interpreted as part of the new study of man and his art. The discovery of cultures different to our own resulted in a rationalization of their lifestyles in terms of Western experiences. However, because of traders' romanticized accounts of the East, and because trade was predominantly in luxuries, very little was known about life in China or Japan, or of the history of the countries and their art, until the end of the nineteenth century.

The fact that there was an enormous difference between Chinese decorative arts made for trade and for the domestic market was not generally realized in the West until after the sacking by British and French troops of the Summer Palace in Beijing in 1860 and the flooding of auction rooms in Paris and London with imperial treasures. In 1884 the Museum was given a gold ewer by Lady Hope Grant which had been presented to her husband Lieutenant General Sir Hope Grant, GCB, by his command, with an inscription stating they had bought it at the sale of the loot of the Summer Palace. It is probable that many of the high quality Ming and Qing carved lacquers in the Museum's collection could be traced back through private collectors to this source. The brushpot (page 18) and small round box (left) came to the Museum in the 1930s as part of a

Gold wine ewer from the Imperial Summer Palace at Beijing. Made in 1852.

substantial gift of lacquer by an expatriate Scot, A E Anderson, and over thirty pieces were purchased from the lacquer collection of Lee Yu-kuan in the early 1960s.

The imperial treasures revealed true Chinese art and taste, and stimulated a desire in many Westerners to understand Chinese culture and aesthetics. Progress was slow, however, and it was not until the preparations for the Chinese Art exhibition at the Royal Academy in 1935 that Chinese connoisseurs and their European counterparts began seriously to discuss the subject. At last Europeans had the chance to explore works of art that they had previously viewed superficially, and to learn something of the traditions of the Chinese connoisseur. However, despite increasing interest in Chinese art, scholarship has been hindered by the linguistic barrier and by China's relative political

Group of nineteenth-century Japanese ivory netsuke.

isolation since 1949. These factors have also affected contact between Chinese and European artists and craftsmen in the twentieth century.

The situation with regard to Japanese art is somewhat different. An aesthetic dialogue had existed between Japan and Europe from the 1860s which initiated an earlier understanding and flourishing of cross-cultural influences. The greater accessibility of Japan at this time was the result of a closer and more equal trade partnership than that with China. With the industrial revolution and the advent of mass-produced goods, Europe could now make many items, such as porcelain, more cheaply than importing them from China. In contrast, Western trade with Japan was set to burgeon.

A strong, central government was emerging in Japan and took power under the Meiji restoration of 1868. At first foreigners were restricted to treaty ports but were soon able to reside in Tokyo and Osaka. Although anti-foreign feeling had fuelled the nationalist current that led to the restoration of the Meiji emperor, the new rulers were determined to modernize Japan along Western lines. They employed many foreign experts, replacing them with Japanese as soon as they had learned all they could. By 1899 Japan could begin to claim equality with the West.

The Museum was given large collections of Japanese sword furniture and *netsuke*, particularly between 1890 and 1946. These were originally amassed at the end of the nineteenth century when interest in miniature art from Japan was at its height. In 1887 the Museum bought a collection of over three thousand prints in albums and rolls. Mostly from the late eighteenth and nineteenth century, there are some rarities, and many prints retain their original colours. Purchases have also been made from various important collections.

It was not until the late 1870s and 1880s that appreciation of Japanese art of the earlier periods began in earnest. This mood of growing discrimination and mutual understanding was reflected in the Japan-British exhibition of 1910 where a retrospective section illustrated, for the first time in the West, the greatest Japanese artists from all periods. This exhibition was the crowning expression of friendship between the two countries, whose diplomatic relationship had been cemented with the Anglo-Japanese alliances of 1902 and 1905. Although the British were at first unsure how to treat a non-Western nation as an equal partner, one area where the new relationship flourished was the arts. Japanese graphic artists absorbed influences from the West, to the great benefit of twentieth-century graphic art in Japan, and British potters, such as Bernard Leach, learned much from the Japanese. After studying in Japan, Leach set up his own pottery in England which to this day remains a link between East and West.

By putting on permanent display its collections of Chinese, Japanese and Korean art, the Museum hopes to foster more such links between East and West. The collections inevitably reflect the early European taste in luxuries, but continuing scholarship and increased access to the East have allowed the Museum to develop them in ways that should give the visitor a deeper understanding than Marco Polo had of the cultures that produced them.

LACQUER

Lacquer is unique to the Far East. For this reason lacquerware has always been regarded as a luxury, one that never ceases to intrigue the onlooker because of the complexities involved in its manufacture. The Museum has a splendid and comprehensive collection of lacquerware which displays the artistic and technical virtuosity achieved in a medium foreign to the West.

Lacquer is the sap of a tree, *Rhus verniciflua*, indigenous to China and Japan. The tree was cultivated as lacquer provides an ideal protective coating for items made of wood, bamboo, leather and cloth. Once dry, lacquer is resistant to water and, to some extent, heat. A lacquer coating is made up of many thin layers of raw lacquer, each of which must be no more than 0.03 mm thick in order for it to dry and remain solid as progressive layers are built up. Each layer takes several days, even weeks, to dry, depending on the temperature and humidity. The drying time means that many carved lacquers of the Ming dynasty (1368-1644), to which as many as two hundred layers were applied, must have taken well over a year to make. The process was often prolonged by exploiting the layered surface to decorative effect: designs were carved or inlaid into the surface, or the lacquer itself was coloured with pigments such as cinnabar or vermilion for red, orpiment for yellow and an iron compound or carbon for black. The uppermost layers of lacquer might be thickened with ash or a powder made of horn, shell, bone, sandstone or pottery. These complex techniques meant that lacquerware was very costly to produce, and lacquer items great luxuries.

The earliest known Chinese lacquer object is a wooden bowl covered in vermilion lacquer dated to about 4000 BC. Lacquerwares have been found at sites in China dating from the Shang (*c*1600-*c*1050 BC) and the Zhou (*c*1050-221 BC) periods, but the earliest lacquer in the Museum is an eared cup (overleaf) made in the Western Han period (206 BC-AD 9). By the Han period there were official workshops responsible for the manufacture of lacquer for the imperial household, but the Museum's eared cup was probably made privately by a lacquer craftsman for an individual. Oval in shape, with two elongated flat lip handles, the cup is of wood, lacquered black on the outside, the rim and the centre of the inside, and red on the rest of the inside. A number of similar cups were excavated from the Western Han tombs at Mawangdui, near Changsha in Hunan province. Fifty of these cups were inscribed with the words *jun feng shi* (to serve

Detail of Japanese lacquered wooden box showing fans on the lid. The fans are decorated in sprinkled gold flakes in lacquer, and raised gold takamakie, *on a wood grain* mokume *background. Dated 1714.*

you food), and forty with the words *jun feng jiu* (to serve you wine). The inscription on this eared cup gives the name of the lacquering technique, *jiachu* (fabric body) and contains the character *hao* which indicates that the cup was made for burial in a tomb. The name in the inscription, Yuan ma, is likely to be that of the owner rather than that of one of the lacquer craftsmen, as the latter were not regarded as artists and tended to remain anonymous. *Jiachu* is a technique in which the basic model of wood or metal is covered with fabric such as hemp, linen or silk resulting in a stronger core.

Lacquer production declined at the end of the Eastern Han dynasty (AD 25-220) as pottery and porcelain gradually replaced lacquer for serving food and wine. However, undecorated lacquer plates and vessels were again in use by the Tang dynasty in northern China (618-906) and their use may have continued to the eighteenth century, although the best known examples date from the Song dynasty (960-1279). The brown lacquer dish with a six-lobed rim is similar in form to Ding ware porcelain manufactured in the Song dynasty. The rims of many Ding porcelains are bound with copper, and this feature has been imitated on the lacquer dish. It is dated to the eleventh or twelfth century.

Chinese eared cup, made between 206 BC and AD 9, for burial in a tomb. The detail shows the cup's inscription.

The majority of carved lacquers of the Ming and Qing dynasties, that is from the late fourteenth to the early twentieth century, have a wooden core to which many layers of lacquer, sometimes of more than one colour, have been applied. The design has then been carved into the layers of lacquer, revealing the contrasting colours. Within the Museum's group of carved lacquers is a distinct group of dishes, made at the end of the Yuan dynasty (1279-1368), which are known from their design as 'two-bird' dishes. The Museum has two examples of this type, one of carved black lacquer and one of red. The birds are surrounded by flowers and foliage and on the underside of the rim there is a *xiangcao* (fragrant grass) scroll of stylized S-shapes. The red lacquer dish has a buff-coloured layer of lacquer at the base of the carved design.

Some of the carved Ming lacquers bear official inscriptions. Pieces had not been officially inscribed since the end of the Han dynasty, but the practice began again in the Yongle reign (1403–25) of the Ming dynasty. The imperial pieces of the Yongle reign are of high quality red lacquer carved with landscapes and floral designs. Popular items were dishes and circular boxes (page 8). Also bearing an imperial inscription is the woman's tiered

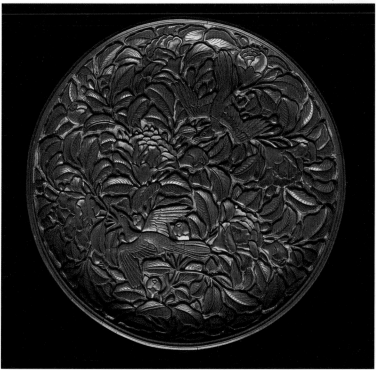

Dish of lacquer, the rim bound with copper. Made in China in the eleventh or twelfth century.

Carved lacquer Chinese 'two-bird' dish from the fourteenth century.

Chinese tiered cosmetic box, carved on the base with the imperial mark of Xuande.

cosmetic box. Pieces made for women at the imperial workshops have inscriptions of only four characters. The two characters referring to the Ming dynasty were omitted, it is said, because of the superstitious belief that the fate of the Ming dynasty should not be left in the hands of a woman. The incised four-character reign mark, filled with gold, on the base dates the box to the reign of Xuande (1426-35). The design of peonies and leaves was carved into the layer of red lacquer until a black 'guide' layer was revealed. Immediately beneath the black layer is a buff ground, exposed by the carving but not carved into. The lid, of deeply carved red lacquer, shows two immortals sitting under a pine tree by a lake.

By building up layers of different-coloured lacquers and carving into them to reveal these different layers, rich, multicoloured objects were produced. One such is the imperial rice measure, which, according to Museum records, was the ceremonial measure used by a palace official to regulate the amount of rice prescribed daily for the emperor. It is perhaps more likely that it was used in one of the many rituals conducted by the emperor to ensure the continuity of the dynasty. On this rice measure, thick layers of red, green and yellow lacquer have been built up and then carved in such a way that the different colours become visible at the edges of the carved motifs. By varying the depth of carving, certain elements of the design have been differentiated by colour: deep carving has produced the green dragons, which lie below the shallower red dragons. Five-clawed dragons are symbolic of the emperor, and are seen here amongst clouds and waves

16

Sixteenth-century Chinese imperial rice measure, perhaps used in rituals to ensure dynastic continuity.

above Meru, the sacred mountain of the Buddhists. Above the dragons on each side is a variant of the character *shou* meaning 'to live for ten thousand years'. On the base of the measure is a six-character reign mark of the Jiajing emperor (1522-66).

Another decorative technique applied to lacquer was inlay. In some cases, incised designs were inlaid with fine gold leaf, a technique known as *qiangjin* (incised, gold-filled). The origins of this technique are unknown, but a square box decorated in this way comes from the tomb of Zhu Ran who died in AD 249. After the Yongle period (1403-25) most inlaid lacquers are decorated by the technique known as *tianqi* (filled-in). The design was incised and filled in with coloured lacquers, and the outlines of the motifs incised and filled with gold. The imperial brushpot (overleaf) is an excellent example of this technique. It is made of wood with red lacquer applied. The main decoration is contained within four panels outlined in black lacquer. The red lacquer has been inlaid with green and yellow lacquers and gold leaf to form a design of two five-clawed imperial dragons on each side of a stylized form of the character for longevity, *shou*. A delicate, finely-incised, so-called cash diaper pattern, one of several characteristic designs for filling

in backgrounds, is inlaid with gold by the *qiangjin* technique. An eight-character reign mark on the base dates the brushpot to 1602 in the Wanli period of the Ming dynasty.

Also bearing an eight-character reign mark is the rare incense stand, dated to 1623 in the reign of the Tianqi emperor, the penultimate emperor of the Ming dynasty. The stand, probably one of a pair, combines the incised and inlaid techniques. The design motifs are outlined in gold leaf and filled with polychrome lacquers. Although the top is decorated with an imperial dragon, the sides, legs and base are engraved and inlaid with flowering peony and prunus amongst foliage. The incense stand, the eared cup, the tiered cosmetic box and the two-bird dishes came to the Museum with thirty-one other pieces from the collection of Lee Yu-kuan, a pioneer in the study of lacquer. The other pieces described belong to the group of lacquers donated to the Museum between 1928 and 1935 by A E Anderson.

In addition to small lacquer items the Museum also has three pieces of lacquer furniture. Donated in 1950, these two thrones and a chair are said to have come from the Summer Palace in Beijing after it was sacked in 1860. The larger throne, made in the Kangxi period (1662–1722), was exhibited at the Burlington Fine Arts Club in 1915. The back and arms of the eighteenth-century throne (overleaf) are removable, making this large piece of furniture portable. Of particular interest are the interiors of its arms which have small shelved alcoves to hold personal treasures such as jade carvings. These can only be reached easily by sitting on the deep seat of the throne. The aesthetic and tactile qualities of small objects of jade, lacquer, bronze or porcelain were greatly appreciated by the Chinese who had collected such objects since the Song period (960–1279).

Brushpot, made in China and dated on the base to 1602.

Incense stand, made in China in 1623.

Eighteenth-century throne, taken from the Summer Palace at Beijing in 1860.

The throne is made of black lacquered wood painted in various shades of gold. Red has been used to outline the designs on many areas of the throne, giving the gold a warm, luminous quality. The seat has a circular medallion in which clouds surround a five-clawed fully-faced dragon and the sacred jewel. Bats, with stylized leaf scrolls in their mouths, fly amongst peonies around the central medallion. The back of the throne has stylized swastikas carved in high relief against a gold leaf ground on each side of the central panel. This bears the musical stone known as a *qing*, surrounded by five bats bringing the five blessings of longevity, peace, riches, a love of virtue and a happy death. The painted gold designs on the back and sides of the throne are of freely drawn landscapes with small rocky islands, trees sheltering pavilions, against a background of waves. The combination of abstract and naturalistic designs on this piece of furniture is characteristic of the period of the Qianlong emperor (1736-95).

The earliest known Korean lacquers date from the first century BC and are writing brush holders and food containers of similar shape to early Korean pottery dishes. They are lacquered black and are easily distinguishable from contemporaneous decorated lacquers imported from Han China. Decorated lacquers manufactured in Korea have been found from the time of King Munyong of Paekche (sixth century AD). Wooden pillows and footrests painted with lacquer designs within thin strips of gold laid in hexagonal patterns may have been influenced by trade contacts with the Southern dynasties (AD 265-589) of China. However, the development of this style in Korea is very different from its original Chinese form in which objects were decorated with thin gold sheets cut into the form of birds and animals.

During and after the Koryo period (935-1392) the characteristic decoration on Korean lacquerware is a combination of mother of pearl and tortoiseshell inlay. The Museum has a superb eighteenth-century example of this technique. The coiled dragon on the top of the round food box winds down onto the sides as if it were curled around it. The dragon is inlaid in mother of pearl and tortoiseshell on a brown lacquer background which has been sprinkled with gold and covered in several layers of transparent lacquer. Inside the box a rich textural design of phoenixes is achieved by using mother of pearl, tortoiseshell, and sharkskin inlay against a background of gold-speckled brown lacquer. The designs are further enhanced by twisted copper wire which emphasizes certain outlines and scrolls.

The first Japanese lacquered objects to reach Europe were portable chests and coffers in the sixteenth century. The sprinkled gold and silver designs, often with inlaid mother of pearl against a black lacquer background, were very popular, and the term 'japanned' came into use for objects varnished in imitation of oriental lacquers.

In contrast to the carved lacquers of China the form of the object being decorated in Japan is paramount and great attention is given to two-dimensional decoration. Lacquer objects with simple painted designs have been dated to the neolithic period in Japan. A number of red and black lacquered wooden bowls and red lacquer combs were found at the Torihama shell mound in Fukui province with pottery dating to the fourth millennium BC. Hundreds of excavation finds, especially in eastern Japan, illustrate how lacquer

Eighteenth-century lacquer box, an example of the use in Korean lacquerwork of tortoiseshell and mother of pearl inlay.

was used to preserve and decorate caskets, arrows and personal items such as jewellery, from the end of the Jōmon period, c300 BC.

The spread of Buddhism to Japan from China and Korea in the sixth century AD brought with it craftsmen from these countries to build and furnish new temples. The following two centuries brought about changes in the use of lacquer in Japan that are reflected in the fine artistic tradition known today. The inlaid designs of thin sheets of silver and gold, mother of pearl and crystal, found on objects belonging to Emperor Shomu (701-756), reflect Chinese Tang dynasty style and techniques. Although such techniques were to die out in China, they were further developed in Japan, and a distinctive Japanese style evolved.

Sprinkled picture (*makie*) lacquer was first made in the Heian period (794-1185). This technique involved the sprinkling of silver and gold filings onto a lacquer ground before it had completely hardened. Several types of *makie* were developed but the earliest and most complex, known as *togidashi* (polished sprinkled design), was used extensively in the Heian period. Several coats of black lacquer were applied over the decoration and then carefully polished down with charcoal until the sprinkled picture reappeared. The sprinkled picture is therefore at the same level as the surrounding lacquer. Sometimes a layer of transparent lacquer was added for protection.

In the eighteenth century *togidashi* was often combined with other techniques. It can be seen on an eighteenth-century *inrō* in the Museum. *Inrō* were tiered medicine cases used by Japanese men for carrying personal seals and herbs. The Museum's small, four-tiered lidded case has a design of gold bamboo trellis heavily laden with wisteria. Some of the silver blossoms are in *togidashi*, others are of inlaid mother of pearl. The nine-teenth-century *inrō* have designs in *togidashi makie* of a carp ascending a waterfall in gold, brown and silver, and of chrysanthemums in red, silver and gold.

Sprinkled gold was applied to decorate lacquer in two other techniques also seen on *inrō*. A flat sprinkled design (*hiramakie*) is the simplest and most commonly used. Thin sheets of gold and silver or filings are laid or sprinkled on the wet ground lacquer. When dry this is covered with layers of transparent lacquer, with the flat finished design raised slightly above the surrounding lacquer. The gold bamboo trellis on one of the *inrō* and the eight views of Biwa lake near Kyoto on another, decorated in shades of gold, brown, black and silver *hiramakie*, illustrate this technique. Sprinkled pictures were also created in relief (*takamakie*). This technique developed in the fourteenth century in an attempt to represent nature more realistically. A picture was built up using lacquer and charcoal to achieve three-dimensional mountains, rocks or animals. Gold and silver foil and filings were then sprinkled over these forms giving a rich effect. The standing and grazing horses on one *inrō* were decorated in gold, brown, black and silver *hiramakie* and *takamakie*; flat sprinkled design and relief are used together.

Five inrō, *made in Japan in the eighteenth and nineteenth centuries.*

Writing box reflecting a trend towards naturalism in takamakie *design in seventeenth-century Japan.*

The Japanese used lacquer to cover everyday objects including tableware and numerous boxes of different sizes, all with a specific purpose: *obi* boxes, kimono boxes, paper boxes, letter boxes and writing boxes. A seventeenth-century box for writing utensils reflects the popularity of naturalistic design in *takamakie* at this period. The rocks and pavilion at the base of a waterfall are rendered in high relief. The pines on the rounded mountains behind disappear into a mist formed of large irregular flakes of gold densely laid onto the lacquer. This technique is known as Kōdaiji *makie* from the name of the temple where several examples are preserved. Although the technique is often reserved for background it can also be used as part of the design.

The inside of the lid, the pen tray and an inkstone with inkwell are lavishly decorated with flights of small birds over reeds in low relief gold and silver. Both the pen tray and inkstone in its tray can be removed to reveal the rich gold-sprinkled interior. Here the lacquer has not been affected by light and the original colour can be seen. The interiors of many Japanese boxes and *inrō* are executed in layers of sprinkled gold and silver flecks. These are sprinkled from a bamboo tube with a cloth filter onto the layers of transparent lacquer while they are still wet, producing a mist of gold and silver suspended at different levels in the lacquer.

Lacquer designs often convey literary and classical allusions. The twenty-four paragons of filial piety, reflecting Confucian ideals, appear on an eighteenth-century lacquer picnic set. One child rushes in front of his father to save him from a tiger, another lies on the ice of a pond to melt it and catch two carp for his mother. Yet another breastfeeds her great grandmother who has lost all her teeth. Some acts of filial piety were aided by the gods: a boy sent to till the fields in the Li Mountains was helped in his task by an elephant. The picnic cabinet has an open frame with a fixed top and base and silver latticework at the sides. It is carried by an enamelled handle probably made in the nineteenth century to replace the original. A four-tiered food box with lid and a box of five trays, each showing a different design, fit into recesses in the base of the frame. The lid of the tray box has two recesses for chased silver alloy *sake* bottles. Five more trays fit into a box placed on a shelf at the top with two *sake* cups on a tray above the food boxes. All the articles are covered in designs executed in high and low relief gold and silver *makie* with mother of pearl and coral inlay on the top to indicate cherry and plum blossoms. In Japan in the spring families and friends still have picnics under the blossoming cherry trees to celebrate the season of rebirth. This picnic set of superior quality would have been used for such occasions.

Eighteenth-century Japanese picnic set.

SILK

The soft, lustrous, yet strong fibre, silk, has long been associated with China. Its name is derived from Latin *sericum*, Greek *serikos*, 'silken', from *Seres*, meaning 'oriental people', probably the Chinese and the Tibetans. These peoples were first encountered by Greeks accompanying Alexander the Great; by the time of the Roman emperor Augustus the Chinese were famous as producers of silk. The Romans obtained great quantities of the material via the Silk Route, the overland trade route that linked China with the Roman empire.

The production of silk became so important to the Chinese economy that a myth developed dating its discovery to the third millennium BC, when the legendary Empress Xiling, wife of Huangdi, the Yellow Emperor, is said to have invented the loom and taught the people how to unwind threads from silkworm cocoons to make into garments. This imperial connection was maintained throughout the dynasties with the reigning empress performing state sacrifices to her deified predecessor every spring.

The earliest examples of silk so far discovered are fragments found in a bamboo basket in Zhejiang province, carbon-dated to *c*2800 BC, about the date accorded to Empress Xiling. Further finds, as well as references in inscriptions on Shang period bronze vessels (*c*1600–*c*1050 BC), and official records of silk production during the Western Zhou dynasty (*c*1050–771 BC), suggest a thriving industry even at this early date. By the Han dynasty (206 BC–AD 220) the Chinese silk industry was well organized, with a sophisticated division of labour and elaborate weaving techniques. For the most part, weaving was concentrated in the southern cities of Hangzhou, Suzhou, Nanjing and Guangzhou (Canton), with tailors and embroidery workshops throughout China. Silks for clothing were embroidered by hand, largely in professional embroidery workshops peopled by women and young girls, although there was a tradition of domestic embroidery for small items.

While silk was a major industry, its production was complex, time consuming and labour intensive. Consequently costs were high and silk was an expensive commodity. Silk is the unwound thread of cocoons made by the larvae of the domestic silkworm, *Bombyx mori*, the only variety of worm that will feed off the picked leaves of the cultivated white mulberry tree, *Morus alba*. The method of harvesting has remained the same for centuries. Each silkworm larva is fed on mulberry leaves for thirty days, during which

Detail of a late nineteenth-century fukusa *or Japanese gift cover.*

Handscroll painting, Fishing in Willow Brook, *by Chinese artist Wang Hui, dated 1706.*

time it increases in size from 2mm to 5cm, consuming twenty times its own body weight in leaves. It then spins a cocoon around itself, in which the transformation into a moth takes place. This process takes about ten days, after which the cocoon is plunged into boiling water, killing the moth and retaining the cocoon intact. The continuous thread of the cocoon is then unwound onto a reel. A single cocoon can provide a thread measuring anything from 500 to 1500 metres. Great care has to be taken to protect the sensitive silkworm from disturbances such as climatic change, pollution, even noise.

Silk has traditionally been used in East Asia not only for clothing and decorative hangings but also as furnishing fabric and a surface for painting, like a canvas. Silk for painting on was specially prepared with various primers such as glucose solution, starch, glue and alum, after which it was ready for ink and watercolours. Silk was also used in the mounting of paintings in horizontal or vertical scroll format. A scroll was rolled around a dowel: bottom to top for a hanging scroll and left to right for a handscroll. Once rolled, it was secured by a semicircular rod with two ivory or bone pins attached by a length of silk. As well as a silk mount, paintings also had end sections covered with contrasting silks, usually patterned or brocaded. Handscrolls were unrolled from right to left with only a small section viewed at a time. Illustrated here is a handscroll in ink and colours on silk by the eminent artist Wang Hui (1632-1717) and his pupil Yang Jin (1644-1728), dated 1706. Dedicated to its subject, Wang Jing Bo, the artistic or 'fancy' name of the artists' fellow painter Wang Kui, it shows him enjoying the pleasures of fishing, surrounded by scholarly accessories: inkstone, brush, brushwasher, incense burner, books, scrolls and a vase of flowers. He is attended by a servant preparing refreshments.

Paintings could also be mounted in album form. Below are two leaves from a part album of sixty-five painted silk folios called the *Huangchao liqi tushi* (Illustrated Precedents for the Ritual Paraphernalia of the Imperial Court). Commissioned by the Qianlong emperor (1736-95) in 1759, the complete Illustrated Precedents consisted of over twenty volumes, each containing thirty folios, and provide a visual and descriptive record of the court ceremonial dress of the emperor and imperial family, the official dress of civil and military officials, and the ritual paraphernalia for ceremonial occasions. These two leaves show, as indicated by the title in the top right-hand corner, the front of the emperor's silk Winter Court Robe No 2, which, with its otter-fur trim was worn in the late autumn, and the reverse of the emperor's silk Winter Court Robe No 1, trimmed in sable and worn at the beginning of the winter. Apart from their brilliant yellow colour, which was reserved exclusively for the emperor and close family members, these court robes or *chaofu* denote their imperial status by the presence of the Twelve Symbols (Sun, Moon, Constellation, Mountain, Dragon, Pheasant, Symbol of Discretion, Axe, Sacrificial Cups, Waterweed, Fire and Grain) interspersed amongst the clouds and five-clawed dragons. As the title Winter Robe suggests, the dress of the emperor and other members of the imperial family was regulated by the time of year and sometimes also by function.

Most of the Chinese clothing surviving in Western museum collections dates from the Qing dynasty (1644-1911) and much is of silk. Everyday formal dress for Qing

Two painted silk folios executed about 1759, showing two of the court robes of the Chinese emperor.

imperial officials consisted of a silk dragon robe (*longpao*), worn with accessories such as a surcoat, rank badge, high boots, a string of beads and a hat. As the Qing were Manchus, the cut of the dragon robe derived from a nomadic tradition that had developed a tailored garment, with the skirt section split at the back and front for riding horseback, and close-fitting sleeves with horse-shoe cuffs. Although the colour of a robe could vary, as could the number of auspicious symbols, its cut and the design of, usually nine, dragons in clouds over a sea and mountains tended to be standardized, so that the example illustrated here is typical of robes worn until the end of the Chinese imperial system in 1911. Many of the accessories worn with the dragon robe, such as the rank badge attached to the

Nineteenth-century pith painting showing a Chinese Qing dynasty official wearing full official dress.

Dragon robe, necklace, hat and boots, and rank badge from a surcoat worn by Chinese Qing dynasty officials. Late nineteenth century.

front and back of the surcoat and the finial on the hat, denoted the wearer's position within the official hierarchy. There were nine ranks in both the civil and the military bureaucracies, differentiated by birds and animals respectively.

A hat was an indispensable part of official dress and during the Qing dynasty two types were worn: a conical bamboo hat in the summer months and a fur-brimmed hat in the winter. It is likely that the shape of the winter hat evolved from Manchu-style headgear, with the fur brim once worn down over the ears to protect the head from the cold. The Museum's winter hat is a typical example: a close-fitting cap with a padded crown covered with red silk cording fixed at the apex of the hat, and an upturned brim faced with fur. Individual rank was determined by a jewel attached to the top of the hat. The nine ranks, both civil and military, were denoted by differently coloured jewels.

Officials could be awarded additional distinctions, equivalent to medals and decorations bestowed in the West. One was the right to wear a peacock feather (*ling zhi*), which was conferred by the emperor. This was attached to the hat by means of a tube made of jade, or similar hardstone, and a metal fitting. The triple-eyed peacock feather was restricted to imperial princes of the first three ranks and the double-eyed feather to lower ranking Manchu nobles. The single-eyed peacock feather (*dan yan hua ling*), page 30, was awarded to Chinese nobles and officials down to the sixth rank.

Informal robes were free of any decorative uniformity, although the cut of garments would generally be the same and, for women, there was a repertoire of motifs appropriate to the wearer's age and the time of year when the robe was worn. Men's informal dress tended to be relatively plain, while that of women was highly colourful and often elaborately embroidered. As a rule, dress for Han Chinese and Manchu women differed: Han women favoured a short jacket and trousers, over which was worn a wrap-around skirt, while Manchu women preferred a full-length robe. The Manchu woman's silk *kesi* (tapestry weave) robe, which dates from the late nineteenth century, is decorated in a style favoured by the Empress Dowager Cixi (1835-1908). A similarly decorated gauze robe associated with Cixi is in the Royal Ontario Museum. Although there is no evidence that this robe was made for her, it is possible that she established a fashion for these robes with bold realistic flowers and stylized *wanshou* (live for ten thousand years) characters. An accomplished painter of birds and flowers herself, Cixi or one of her court painters may have provided the original designs for this style of robe, and indeed for a group of porcelains in a similar style, made in celebration of her sixtieth birthday in 1894 (by Chinese reckoning). The longevity characters signify that the robe was made for an older woman and the design of chrysanthemums indicates that the robe was made for autumn wear.

Manchu woman's robe, worn in China in the late nineteenth century, with designs favoured by the Empress Dowager Cixi.

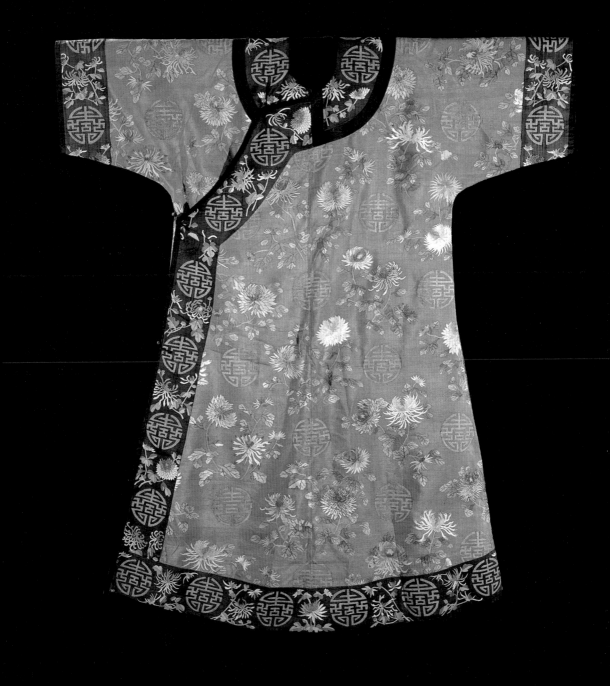

Eighteenth-century silk altar frontal made in China, probably for the Catholic market.

Silk was an important export commodity, one that China traded with its immediate Asian neighbours as well as with India, the Near East and Europe. European trade with China peaked during the eighteenth century when tea and silk cloth were the major cargoes carried by the English, Dutch, Swedish, Danish and other East India companies. However, finished silk objects were largely the private trade of ships' officers and merchants who took commissions on behalf of individuals and dealers. It is possible that the Museum's elaborately embroidered altar frontal of about 1740 was a commission for the European market, although it could have been made for Jesuits operating in China or Japan, or have formed part of the speculative trade in religious vestments and hangings for Catholic missions in the Philippines and Spanish Americas.

The introduction of sericulture to Japan from China via Korea is shrouded in myth. It seems likely that Japanese military expeditions into Korea in the fourth century AD returned with weavers. The consequent arrival of seeds of the mulberry bush and silk-worm eggs led to the establishment of silk production. Silk was worn only at the court or reserved for tax and tribute until Buddhism was introduced in the mid-sixth century and pictorial representations of the Buddha were made in silk tapestry and embroidery. Buddhist ritual and ceremony also entailed the use of silk banners and garments.

Though it is said that in the fifth century a more ordinary quality of silk was woven in Japan in an effort to popularize its use, silk remained the preserve of the aristocracy at court and in the temple until the rise of the military clans in the twelfth century. It was at this time that the multilayered full kimono worn over the *hakama*, a long pleated skirt, popular in the Heian period (794-1185), was replaced by the *kosode*, a simpler garment with shorter sleeves worn inside the *hakama*. This new dress of the women of the warrior class reflected the emphasis placed on frugality by the feudal lords. The modern kimono developed from this *kosode*. During the Muromachi period (1333-1568) the *hakama* disappeared from female dress and a long outer robe, the *uchikake*, was used for formal occasions. This robe has been adopted as bridal wear in traditional Japanese wedding ceremonies.

The *kosode* grew to ankle length and a sash was required to hold the front together, previously achieved by tucking the *kosode* into the *hakama*. At first the *obi*, as this sash came to be known, was very simple and made of braided cords. In the eighteenth century attention shifted gradually from the design of the kimono to that of the *obi* which became wider and was tied in many different styles.

A kimono is made of straight strips of silk, each about half a metre in width. Woven silk, heavy silk crepe, spun silk and silk gauze were sold in lengths sufficient to make a kimono or an *obi*. The silk was either dyed before it was sold, or was sold as white fabric for the application of hand-painted designs (*yūzen*) or stencils, or for dyeing by one of the resist dye techniques. The silk crepe *furisode* overleaf is a type of kimono with long sleeves worn by unmarried women. It has a padded hem and a colourful design, both of which date it to the second half of the Meiji era (1868-1912), when kimonos enjoyed a vivid renaissance. Worn much looser than today, the kimonos of this time often had three layers. Contrasting linings, which could be glimpsed at hem and sleeve, were also popular. This kimono is three-quarter lined in scarlet silk. The design of the upper half of the kimono was often different in motifs and composition from that of the lower half, though related in theme, and patterns were chosen for their appropriateness to the season. Here spring is evoked, in the lower half of the kimono and sleeves by the design of peony bushes blooming rather early under their snow-capped protective straw covers, and in the upper half by sparrows flying among branches covered with plum blossom. The two design elements would be separated by the wide *obi* when the kimono was worn.

Designs were hand drawn in ink which was later washed out. The areas to be dyed were outlined in resist so that the colours would not bleed. Steaming set the colours which were then covered in resist and the background colour applied with a brush.

Finally the whole was steamed and washed. Aspects of this design are picked out with embroidery: the yellow French knots emphasize the centres of the flowers, and self-coloured stem stitch gives texture to some of the pink petal edges.

The *obi* or sash was, and still is, often the most expensive item of a woman's dress. The most elegant are of brocade, handwoven in the Nishijin district of Kyoto. The double-sided sash is from the Taishō era (1912-26). Its rectangular length has been folded along the warp to form a double thickness of weft-faced brocade, hand-sewn on three sides. This type of sash, known as a *maru obi*, is worn with formal and semi-formal kimonos but is particularly popular for bridal kimonos in which case it would be decorated with gold and silver threads.

Men's kimonos developed from the multilayered robes worn over trailing loose trousers into the formal wear of the samurai which has remained the basis of men's formal kimonos today. A striped silk *hakama,* a form of pleated divided skirt, is worn over a black silk kimono, and a *haori*, a three-quarter-length loose jacket with sleeves, is put on over the top. Previously a sleeveless, open-fronted, long waistcoat with stiff wings of fabric at the shoulders was worn. This form of dress was known as a *kamishino* and became popular in the eighteenth century. Informally men dressed in full-length kimonos with a stiff or soft *obi* tied at the back of the waist, and this style of dress is still worn by some in the evenings or at summer festivals.

Double-sided obi *or sash, made in Japan between 1912 and 1926.*

Boy's underkimono dating from the 1930s, showing detail of the stencilled relief pattern on the lower part.

The garment worn under a male kimono, known as a *nagajuban*, may be more elaborately decorated than the kimono itself. The upper part of this silk underkimono, made in the 1930s, is woven in a process commonly known as ikat, but called *kasuri* in Japan. This technique, in which the threads of floss silk are dyed before being woven, is explained in the chapter on cotton. The flamboyant pattern indicates that it was probably made to celebrate the boys' festival held on 5 May each year. The Japanese characters are those for horse and desire. Designs of horses reflect the owner's valour. The way in which the characters are placed on shaped panels suggests the wooden boards of similar shape known as *ema* (horse), sold at Japanese shrines and temples. Visitors to the temple put their name, the date and their specific plea on an *ema* before hanging it in a designated place. In the past horses were a traditional offering to temples and the name of the wooden board is derived from this custom.

In present-day Japan Western clothes are the norm for everyday wear, and Japanese designers such as Issey Miyake provide an exciting synthesis of East and West. The traditional kimono is still worn, however, at festivals and for special occasions, and by a few of the older generation, particularly in Kyoto, on a daily basis.

Perhaps one of the most colourful silk items in Edo period Japan (1600-1868) was the *fukusa* or gift cover used in the exchange of gifts. These covers were often embroidered in silks and gold thread with designs appropriate to the occasion of their use. Gifts were placed on a tray with the *fukusa* either folded or laid over the gift with the design towards the inside and the lining, often embroidered with a family crest, exposed. On receipt of the gift the *fukusa* was admired and taken with the tray and gift from the room. A small gift replaced the original on the tray, the *fukusa* was laid over it and the whole returned to the giver. Differences in the construction of *fukusa* lie in the form of the tassels and the way in which the lining and decorative panel are joined together. The red crepe lining of this satin *fukusa* forms a border on the front, and tassels were attached at the four corners; one is now missing. The tassels are of a style typical of the late Edo period. The design worked in gold and coloured silks refers to an incident in the life of Shiba Onkō, an eleventh-century Chinese statesman. In his childhood he saved the life of a friend who had fallen into a large jar of water by breaking the jar with a rock. This Confucian legend had been popular in Japan since the fourteenth century and this scene illustrates the proverb 'genius displays itself even in childhood'. This *fukusa* would have been used in a ceremony relating to children. *Fukusa* can still be bought in Japanese department stores, where videos are shown to instruct the customer on the etiquette of their use, which is nowadays mainly only on very formal occasions or in corporate entertaining.

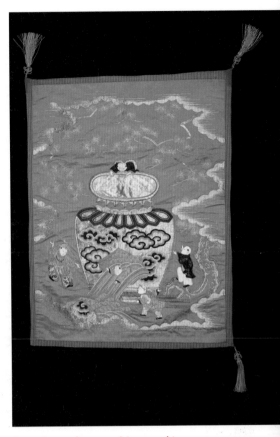

Late nineteenth-century fukusa *used in the formal presentation of gifts in Japan.*

POTTERY

Pottery is the term used to describe articles made of earthenware or baked clay. Pottery items are baked or fired in a kiln at low temperatures, up to about 1000°C. This is what distinguishes them from porcelain, which is fired at very high temperatures. Strictly speaking, stoneware is made of a material closer to that used for porcelains, a clay with a high proportion of silica, and for this reason Chinese stoneware is dealt with in the chapter on porcelain. However, the stoneware of Japan is discussed here together with earthenware as the two fall within the same tradition, one quite separate from the porcelain tradition which developed only in the seventeenth century in Japan.

The earliest Chinese earthenwares, dating from c7000 BC in the neolithic period, were utilitarian vessels of coarse red clay fired at low temperatures. These were produced first in the southwest and later in the north of China. The earliest known large-scale ceramic producing culture was the Peiligang of north China (c6500 BC) who made jars, bowls, cups, urns and small animal sculptures from a coarse, sandy clay. The Yangshao culture of northwest China (c5000-3000 BC) began to use a more sophisticated, finely levigated clay. The earliest Yangshao excavation, at Banpo, yielded a variety of shapes of vessel used for storage and for burial, and the earliest pottery so far known to be decorated with images of fish, no doubt an important food source for the community. The archaeological site of Banpo revealed a village divided into living areas, a cemetery and ceramic kilns. In about 3000 BC, the east coast Longshan culture developed its own black earthenware. This finely made ware benefited from the use of the potter's wheel, invented during the fourth millennium BC.

A later development of the Yangshao culture, further west in Gansu province, and known as the Gansu Yangshao, took place between 3000 and 1500 BC and can be divided into three main phases: the Majiayao, the Banshan and the Machang. In the Museum's collection and illustrated overleaf is a typical example of a storage jar of the Banshan type with a globular red earthenware body, thinly potted and made by building up horizontal coils of clay which were then smoothed out to become invisible. It would have been fired along with many more in a simple updraft kiln, in which the firebox was situated well below the chamber containing the vessel. The heat of the fire was carried up gradually through a perforated floor, allowing the vessels to dry out before firing. After firing

Detail of an earthenware tomb pillar with stamped relief decoration. Made in China in the Han dynasty (206 BC-AD 220).

Earthenware storage jar made from coiled clay in Gansu province, China, about 2500 BC.

at a low temperature the completed vessel was burnished and the characteristic swirling pattern painted on with unfired black and red mineral pigments.

During the Shang dynasty (*c*1600-*c*1050 BC) the use of glaze, a glassy protective layer applied to the surface of a ceramic, was discovered, probably through ash falling on pots during firing and forming a thin covering. This was a major advance, as glaze was functional, making the porous body of earthenware vessels impervious to liquids, and also providing a decorative finish. Glazed earthenwares were developed for everyday use throughout the succeeding Western and Eastern Zhou periods (*c*1050-221 BC). However, the Eastern Zhou period saw a new category of earthenware: *mingqi* or burial pottery. This was made specifically to be buried in tombs, so that the deceased could enter the afterlife equipped with the items that had been essential to them in life. Many pieces replaced objects normally made of more expensive materials, such as bronze. The best known example of burial pottery is the enormous army of lifesize warriors and horses buried with the emperor Qin Shihuang, who unified China in 221 BC. These were a substitute for the human and animal attendants sacrificed to accompany royal burials in the Shang dynasty.

By the Han dynasty (206 BC–AD 220) burial pottery of humbler proportions and of subject matter reflecting everyday life was widespread. Earthenware models of people, animals, everyday objects such as cooking stoves, and buildings such as granaries, pigpens and farmyards were designed to furnish the tombs of the wealthy, to proclaim the position and importance of the deceased and to demonstrate the filial respect of the living. During the Han dynasty it was believed that when a person died the soul left the body and became two elements: the *hun* which went to paradise and the *po* which remained in the tomb as a spirit (*gui*). The burial pottery appeased the spirit by providing the wherewithal for existence in the otherworld, and encouraged it to assist the living. In the Museum's collection is a realistic model of a granary showing a figure in the process of milling. The green glaze, which is typical, has developed an iridescence through its long exposure to moisture during burial.

Pottery was used for architectural features such as roof tiles, bricks and pillars. The Han period pillar (overleaf and page 40), moulded from a grey earthenware in the form of a model tower, formed part of the internal structure of a tomb. The interior of a tomb was made up of chambers which resembled real buildings and

Green-glazed tomb model representing a granary with a miller grinding grain, made during the Han dynasty in China.

Earthenware tomb pillar from the Han dynasty, China (detail on page 40).

this pillar probably served as the apex to a doorway to one of these chambers. The elaborate stamped designs show the concern in the Han period for both the everyday - buildings, animals and hunting scenes - and the fabulous, magical and mythological, as represented here by the stylized masks and writhing dragons.

The use of earthenware for funerary wares reached an unrivalled degree of sophistication in the Tang dynasty (618-906). Spectacular funerary pieces reflected the cosmopolitan nature of a period of unparalleled growth in trade between China and Western Asia. Carefully observed models of horses, camels and supernatural figures were conspicuously inspired by this trade, as was the vivid three-colour (*sancai*) glaze introduced in the seventh century and whose colours, green, amber and cream, were probably derived from dyed textiles that came, via the Silk Route, from Central Asia. Complex figures were made in a number of moulds, the parts being luted together before glazing and firing. The colours were made by adding metal oxides such as copper and iron to a low-fired lead-flux glaze. The magnificent tomb guardian (*zhenmu shou*) was one of a pair placed in a tomb to protect the deceased. Its dramatic and menacing presence would have been enhanced by the unglazed areas being painted with unfired mineral pigments to give a more demonic appearance. Unlike the *sancai* glaze, this paint rarely survived burial. After the Tang dynasty, elaborate burials were discouraged and earthenware was largely superseded in China by porcelain. Earthenware continued to be used for architectural accessories.

The history of pottery in Japan is quite different, and its influence further reaching. Recent archaeological studies have established the date of the earliest Japanese pottery as *c*10,000 BC. The earliest fragments are of Jōmon (cord pattern) ware, although the patterns, made by rolling sticks wrapped in twisted cord over the surface of the pot, do not appear until about 7500 BC. All Jōmon pots are made from coils of clay pressed together, smoothed with a paddle into a continuous surface, left to dry and finally baked in an open fire. This is the same method of modelling used to make the Chinese neolithic jar illustrated on page 42. The first Japanese pots were used mainly for cooking and are characterized by pointed bases enabling them to stand upright among the stones at the centre of the hearth. They have little decoration apart from the occasional pattern made with a fingernail. Jōmon ware developed to include a variety of vessel shapes, including jars with elaborate high relief patterns and raised rims which may have been used in religious ceremonies. The later phases of Jōmon pottery (c2500-1000 BC) are represented by more utilitarian shapes with decoration restrained to curvilinear patterns and raised bands.

The Museum acquired a number of Jōmon wares from Gordon Munro, a Scottish doctor who lived in Japan at the turn of the century. Munro sent several crates of archaeological specimens from Japan to the Museum, forming the largest collection of its type in Britain. It also includes pottery from the succeeding Yayoi (c300 BC-cAD 300) and Kofun periods (cAD 300-mid sixth century). The pottery of the Yayoi period is also made from coils of clay. The surface was smoothed by trimming and burnishing and the pots were fired to a higher temperature, resulting in a warm red colour. Most of the vessels are bulbous with narrow necks, typical of pots used for the storage of grain. The cultivation of millet and rice was introduced from China at about this period.

The Kofun or Tumulus period is named after the *kofun* or huge mounds that served as tombs for the ruling class. Clay cylinders and

Earthenware tomb guardian from an elaborate burial of the Tang dynasty, China.

figures mounted on hollow cylindrical bases (*haniwa*), made of soft red earthenware comparable to Yayoi pottery, were inserted into the ground in circles around the tomb mounds. Potters' guilds called *haji-bi* were formed to produce *haniwa* and a rough domestic ware of the same porous low fired red earthenware.

Some of the grave goods of the Kofun period provide evidence of the advances in kiln technology that took place at this time. A new type of thin grey stoneware was fired at a higher temperature (up to 1200°C) and was therefore non-porous. Higher temperatures were achieved in a sloping kiln that was tunnelled into the hillside. The flow of air through the kiln could be controlled so that only a small amount of oxygen entered. The amount of oxygen in a kiln controls the colour of earthenware: if there is a large amount the unglazed ware is red; if the oxygen is reduced, it is grey.

Grey stoneware continued to be produced in regular forms with globular bodies and trumpet-shaped mouths. It bears strong similarities to contemporaneous Korean pottery of the Silla period (668-935), suggesting that the new kiln technology and the use of the potter's wheel may have been introduced from Korea to Japan. However, the practice of coiling and beating with textured paddles continued in Japan, and the use of the wheel seems to have been restricted to the trimming and shaving of pots. Munro gave the Museum Japanese and Korean examples of this grey stoneware. In Korea it was made to be buried with the dead and for use as tableware. In Japan this type of stoneware is known as *sueki* from the word *sueru*, to offer, as it was used in the Kofun period for making offerings to the ancestors at the time of burial. It was also used as tableware by the Japanese aristocracy until the twelfth century.

Changes in the form and decoration of Japanese stoneware from the ninth century show the influence of developments in China. As in China, glazing may initially have occurred accidentally by ash from the wood fuel in the kiln melting on a pot during firing. The effects of ash glazing were sought after by the potters at Sanage, a centre of *sueki* manufacture to the east of present-day Nagoya. These potters were inspired by the fine green-glazed wares made in Yue in Zhejiang province in southern China. The Sanage potters also used a lighter coloured clay with a low iron content and allowed oxygen into the kiln, thereby producing green ash-glazed wares with light buff-coloured bodies. These became so popular that their manufacture spread to other kilns in the area. The Nagoya region was responsible for many of the innovations in stoneware technology in the twelfth century which were to remain popular until the sixteenth century. Three of the most distinctive types of ware were the rough unglazed stoneware bowls and dishes made for everyday use at table instead of the more common earthenware; large unglazed stoneware storage jars made at kilns near the coast such as Tokoname; and a high quality glazed ceramic made in the Seto area, not far from Sanage.

Seto ware was strongly influenced by imported Chinese ceramics and used as a substitute where they were unavailable or too expensive. Seto is well known for its tea caddies, many of which have a lid made of ivory. The thick black, often speckled, glaze

Group of Seto ware tea caddies, made in Japan.

was copied from Jian wares imported from Fujian province in southern China. In Japan these black wares are usually referred to as *temmoku*, the Japanese pronunciation of Tianmu, the mountainous area in China where Jian ware was popular in the Chan (Zen) Buddhist monasteries that played host to Japanese monks. The shapes of Japanese tea caddies are more varied than those imported from China and exhibit a charming individuality. Seto caddies were later copied at kilns elsewhere in Japan.

Since the mid-sixteenth century one of the most powerful influences on Japanese culture, in particular on ceramics, has been the Tea Ceremony. Known in Japanese simply as Chanoyu (hot water for tea), this is an elaborate etiquette which includes the making of a fire and a light meal. Powdered green tea, infused with hot water, had been served in a similar way amongst the élite of the Northern Song dynasty (960-1126) in China. The tea was introduced to Japan at the end of the twelfth century by Zen Buddhist monks returning from study in China, and was first used to keep the monks refreshed during their long meditations and for medicinal purposes. Tea tasting competitions which ended in drunken banquets became popular among the urbanized military élite of the fifteenth century, while in more refined circles the appreciation of the utensils used for the serving and storing of tea, and the setting down of rules for their use, became the main concerns.

The adoption of Zen by the samurai and wealthy merchant classes in Kyoto during the fifteenth century prepared them for the meditative atmosphere of the Chanoyu. Tea drinking and the appreciation of the utensils associated with it evolved into a philosophy centring on a special tea room, designed in harmonious colours and textures that filtered daylight and provided a quiet, peaceful atmosphere. When Shōgun Yorimasa (1443-90) had the first tea house built in the gardens of the Ginkakuji Temple, it marked the beginning of Chadō, 'the way of tea', as a separate philosophy combining Zen and aspects of secular life.

The cultivation of peace and harmony was evident in the design of the tea house, its garden and the path leading to it from the waiting room. The choice of scroll and flower decoration for the alcove (*tokonoma*), and of utensils was made with appropriateness to the season and the occasion. Decoration was austere and restrained, with a cultivated appreciation of texture and patina, the rust on an iron kettle, the thick *temmoku* glaze on a tea bowl. Teamasters were considered arbiters of taste in Japan. Although Chinese ceramics had been used for the Tea Ceremony up to the mid-sixteenth century, the teamaster Sen no Rikyu (1522-91) fostered the appreciation of Japanese ceramics, in particular those with a rustic quality. His patronage of the tea bowls of his contemporary Raku Chōjirō caused this family of potters to remain popular throughout the Edo period and into this century. Raku glazes were the first to be applied to pots in Kyoto, which had no sophisticated pottery industry before this time. Since 1945 the Raku method of making pots and glazes has been practised and modified all over the world.

Traditionally Raku pots are formed by hand and fired individually in purpose-built kilns. The texture of the pot is rough and its form irregular, with a thick body particularly

Two tea bowls with Raku glazes.

suited to keeping the tea warm. The thick lustrous glazes are often black, but can range through dark brown to reddish brown or white depending on the treatment in the kiln. The colours are suspended in a lead solution and fired at a temperature of 1000°C for the black glaze. Salmon-pink Raku is so called because the red body under the glaze shows through. The transparent glazes are occasionally dappled with green or white touches.

Established kilns such as those at Bizen, Shigaraki and Tamba, which had specialized in unglazed stonewares, tried new techniques of glazing on new forms suitable for the Tea Ceremony, particularly fresh water jars and vases. The narrow-necked bottle was made in the eighteenth century at Bizen, near Okayama. It has a characteristic hard, dark red stoneware body with a lustrous brown glaze with olive green and yellow markings. These stonewares were fired for long periods of time in kilns fuelled with wood. The ash built up in the chamber, falling on the pots to melt and create these glossy glazes with random markings.

The influence of the Tea Ceremony on Japanese ceramics cannot be underestimated, and in turn these Japanese ceramics have stimulated the modern studio pottery movement in Europe and North America. In Japan today there is a large community of potters who consider themselves as artists rather than craftsmen.

Eighteenth-century earthenware bottle from Bizen, Japan.

PORCELAIN

The simplest definition of porcelain is that it is made of sophisticated clays fired in kilns at very high temperatures, in excess of 1280°C. This distinguishes porcelain from pottery or earthenware: a simple clay fired at lower temperatures. The advantage of porcelain is that it is more robust than earthenware, and its dense, vitreous body makes it impervious to liquid. The success of Chinese porcelain manufacture partly stems from the fact that China is rich in the types of clay that make good porcelain. The properties of these clays were understood and exploited in China from a very early stage.

China is renowned for its porcelain, Japan less so. The very use of the term 'china' in English to denote porcelain points to the enormous popularity and influence of Chinese porcelain in the West. But while the Chinese porcelains imported by the West were generally regarded as luxury items, often for display only, the function of porcelains in China has always been more practical. Most porcelains were made to be used, whether at court, in the temple or at table.

High-fired ceramics were first made in China at kilns in the coastal provinces of Jiangsu and Zhejiang as early as the Shang dynasty (c1600-c1050 BC). However, it was not until the Sui (AD 589-618) and Tang (618-906) dynasties that the Xing kilns in Hebei province and the Gongxian kilns in Henan, both in northern China, produced a translucent white ware which can be said to be the first porcelain. This was formed largely of kaolin, a white, non-plastic clay whose name is derived from the Gaoling mountain range in Jiangxi province, rich in this particular clay. However, the best known porcelains were manufactured from about the tenth century at Jingdezhen in the southeastern province of Jiangxi where there were copious quantities of a high quality clay known as porcelain stone or *bai dunzi* (little white bricks), to which was added varying amounts of kaolin. Jingdezhen eventually became the most important centre of porcelain production in China.

The most sophisticated high-fired wares with a porcelain or porcellaneous body were produced during the Song dynasty (960-1279), stimulated by an expanded economy and market for luxury goods and by a growth in connoisseurship and collecting on the part of the new class of scholar-officials. Because these scholar-officials themselves required fine quality ceramics, they, along with the merchants who were responsible for distributing the wares, became investors in and patrons of the many kilns in China. This led to

Porcelain moon flask, made in China in the early fifteenth century.

Ding ware dish with incised decoration and qingbai *waterpot with moulded decoration. Twelfth or thirteenth-century China.*

tremendous developments in ceramic technology, in terms of glazes and production techniques. The kiln sites were highly industrialized by the standards of twelfth and thirteenth-century Europe, with a sophisticated division of labour and manufacturing processes involving special manual skills. The kilns themselves were also by this time highly developed. The main type of kiln in northern China is known as the *mantou* (bread roll) kiln due to its domed roof. In the south, dragon kilns predominated, so called because of the way their long structure (up to sixty metres) snaked up a hillside.

Many Song wares depend for their effect on an elegant shape and subtle monochrome glaze. Often the glaze was the only form of decoration; sometimes a piece was enhanced by an incised, carved or moulded design. Two Song period porcelains, one from north and one from south China, demonstrate the most frequent methods of decoration: incising and moulding. The dish was made in the northern province of Hebei at kilns situated at Ding Xian. Ding is the name by which wares of this type are commonly known. Developed from white wares produced at the Xing kilns, during the Tang dynasty, Ding ware is characterized by a transparent ivory-tinged glaze achieved by oxidization (allowing air to enter the kiln during firing). On some bowls and dishes, 'tear-staining', slight thickening where the glaze has run down after dipping, can be seen. Most early Ding pieces, like this one, were carved, but at the beginning of the twelfth century moulding was introduced. Due to the escalating demand for the ware, as well as its increasing thinness, the potters introduced a new technique of firing vessels upside down on the rim. This enabled more pieces to be fired at once in the saggar or container. To protect the unglazed rim a copper alloy strip was added. The waterpot was made at Jingdezhen and is of a type known as *qingbai* (blue-white) ware. *Qingbai* foreshadowed the white porcelain produced at Jingdezhen in later dynasties. It has a bluish hue to the glaze due to the presence of iron oxide and the fact that it was fired under reduction conditions (in a kiln where the oxygen content was restricted). As with Ding ware, carving and incising techniques were used and, later, moulded designs which can be seen on this tiny waterpot, used to pour a measured amount of water onto an inkstone for mixing up ink ground from a solid inkcake or stick.

Most Song dynasty ceramics were made for everyday use in wealthy Chinese households. The tall and the black bowls illustrated (overleaf) were made as tablewares and come from the north and south of China respectively. Jun ware, with its lavender-blue glaze, was made in the north, at Linru near Luoyang and at other kiln sites in Henan province. Because of its wide distribution, Jun ware may have a varied body quality and colour but it is characterized by a thick, viscous glaze with thousands of small gas bubbles suspended within it, giving tremendous depth. Early Jun wares were monochrome, like the tall bowl overleaf, but from the twelfth century a dramatic purple splash was introduced, with the random application by brush of copper oxide. The black bowl was made in the southern coastal province of Fujian, at the Jian kilns, famous for their tea bowls, described in the chapter on pottery. Jian wares are thickly potted with an iron-black glaze designed to produce a variety of effects, ranging from 'hair's fur', a finely streaked glaze created by the natural unmixing of the glaze during the firing, to the type known as 'oil spot' illustrated here, named after the spots resembling oil droplets against a plain black ground.

One of the most influential wares produced in the Song dynasty was the green-glazed ware known in the West as celadon. In the north of China celadons were produced at the Yaozhou kilns in Tongchuan county, Shaanxi province, and generally called northern celadons. Characterized by a grey body covered with a clear olive green or greenish yellow glaze, Yaozhou wares were decorated with carving, incising and, later, moulding. Celadons were also produced in the south of China in Zhejiang province. Called Longquan wares after the main centre of production, these celadons have a grey-to-white body covered with a soft, opaque, greyish green or greyish blue glaze. Both celadons, but especially Longquan wares because the extent of their production lasted well into the Ming dynasty (1368-1644), influenced other ceramic producing cultures, in particular

that of Korea. The influence can be seen in the Koryo dynasty (935-1392) bowl (top left) dating to between 1100 and 1150 and produced at kilns in Cholla province on the southwest coast of the country, close to Zhejiang province where Chinese celadons were produced. Korean potters had been producing celadons since at least the ninth century, when they were emulating Tang period Yue wares, the forerunners of Longquan wares. By the twelfth century their greenwares rivalled Chinese celadons.

While most Song ceramics were restrained in decoration, there were exceptions, including the popular, highly decorated northern ware known as Cizhou. Cizhou is in Ci county, Hebei province, but the ware was made in a host of related kilns in Henan, Shaanxi and other parts of Hebei. Like Longquan celadons, Cizhou wares continued to be made into the Ming dynasty. They are distinguished by their solid forms and a spontaneous decoration in black and white looking forward to the free styles and designs of later underglaze blue and white porcelain from Jingdezhen. A wide variety of decorative techniques was used on Cizhou ware, most executed in slip (liquid clay) beneath a transparent glaze. These include *sgraffiato* (carving a design through one slip to expose another, or the body beneath) and black slip painting on a white slip ground, seen in the Museum's pillow. Unusually for Chinese ceramics, some Cizhou ware is signed by the family of potters who produced it. Made by the Zhang family of Zhangdefu in Henan province during the thirteenth century the pillow depicts an episode from a popular drama of the period.

The number of kilns operating during the Song dynasty declined gradually after the dynasty, pressed by invaders from the north, removed its capital south from Kaifeng to Hangzhou in 1127. During the succeeding Mongol Yuan dynasty (1279-1368), Jingdezhen became the official centre of porcelain production for both home and export markets, its wares going as far as the Near East and, ultimately, Europe. Underglaze cobalt blue decoration was used from the fourteenth century at Jingdezhen and developed to a state of perfection in the early fifteenth century under the Ming dynasty (1368-1644). The moon flask illustrated on page 50 dates to the early fifteenth century and is typical of the refined porcelains of the reigns of the emperors Yongle (1403-25) and Xuande (1426-35), with its magnolia flowers and leaves painted in a vivid blue against a fine-grained white body and smooth 'orange peel' effect glaze.

Ming-style blue and white porcelains were emulated during the succeeding Qing dynasty (1644-1911) and new styles were created. There was a greater use of enamels, painted over the glaze to produce a limitless combination of brilliant colours. Enamel painted wares had to be fired twice, once at a high temperature to fuse the body and clear

Top: *Korean bowl of the Koryo dynasty (left), Jun ware bowl (centre) and Jian ware bowl (right), both from China.*

Bottom: *Thirteenth-century Cizhou-ware pillow depicting an episode from popular drama.*

Chinese porcelain plate, decorated with famille verte *enamels, made about 1700.*

glaze, and again at a lower temperature after the enamels had been applied. Under the second Qing emperor, Kangxi (1662–1722), a range of palettes dominated by specific colours was developed. In the West these were termed *famille verte, famille jaune* and *famille noire* due to the predominant use of green, yellow and black enamels. This plate decorated in *famille verte* enamels shows a shift in decorative design, with new emphasis on images taken from popular novels, dramas and legends. Although pieces such as this were made for the domestic market, many found their way to Europe as part of the growing China trade in tea, silk and other luxury goods.

Technical developments in porcelain production continued during the reigns of Yongzheng (1723-35) and Qianlong (1736-95), when wares from Jingdezhen reached a further level of perfection. The *famille rose* (predominantly pink) palette was introduced at this time, and the *doucai* (dovetailed) technique, first developed in the Xuande period (1426-35) of the Ming dynasty, was revived. The *doucai* technique is illustrated by this bowl decorated with Daoist motifs. In the centre of the bowl, Shoulao the star-god is depicted with a deer and *lingzhi* fungus, symbols of long life. On the outside there are further references to longevity: cranes, a pine tree and the Daoist island of the Immortals in the Eastern Sea. Most *doucai* pieces are of high quality and combine an outline design in underglaze cobalt blue, filled in with coloured enamels over the glaze which dovetail into the outline.

For most of the eighteenth century Europe was the biggest export market with hundreds of thousands of pieces exported yearly via the port of Guangzhou (Canton). At the beginning of the century most export porcelains were Chinese in shape and decorated in Chinese taste, but gradually more and more pieces were made to European models and decorated with European designs. The best of these were dinner services or individual pieces ordered by ships' officers and merchants for their customers at home. The punchbowl (page 58) is decorated with an image from the anti-Scottish print *Sawney in the Boghouse*, published just before the Jacobite Rising of 1745. Sawney wears a tartan kilt, bonnet and jacket, a stereotype favoured by the eighteenth-century London press. The bowl would have been part of a special order by an officer or merchant who would have supplied the porcelain decorators with the original engraving from which the design was copied, and who would have brought back the bowl as part of his private cargo. Made at Jingdezhen and decorated in Guangzhou, this bowl demonstrates the

Eighteenth-century Chinese bowl decorated using the doucai *technique.*

Satirical bowl in a style typical of items exported via the port of Guangzhou, China, to Europe in the eighteenth century.

quality achievable by the middle of the eighteenth century, even in shapes and designs quite unfamiliar to the Chinese.

Porcelain manufacture was a carefully guarded secret on the Chinese mainland for many years, although, as we have seen, Korean potters were producing fine celadons in imitation of Chinese Yue ware from as early as the ninth century. White porcelain ware in shades of infinite variety and delicacy was produced in Korea during the Choson dynasty (1392-1910). Most of the white porcelain found in tombs in Korea comes from China but a large number of shards and a small number of entire vessels come from kilns in the Cholla and Kyonggi provinces of Korea. By the beginning of the fifteenth century Korean potters were making white porcelain with underglaze blue decoration using imported cobalt from the Middle East. Imported cobalt was scarce and expensive, but a

small native source of cobalt was found in the
second half of the fifteenth century. Native
Korean cobalt is characterized by its soft blue-
grey colour.

In 1469 the government encouraged production by rewarding the presentation of blue
and white porcelain to the royal household. By
the seventeenth century it had replaced celadon
ware and was used widely throughout Korean
society, although the pottery industry took
some time to recover after the Japanese inva-
sions of 1592 and 1597 when many Korean
potters were taken to Japan. By 1752 the royal
kiln was established at Punwon-ni, where most
of the Museum's collection of blue and white
was probably made. The kiln ceased production in 1883. Punwon-ni was outside Seoul, on
the Han River, where there was access to fire-
wood and good river transport to the capital.
The town attracted cultivated people who
employed painters to design pots, ensuring the
popularity of blue and white porcelain.

The introduction of Chinese porcelain to
Japan appears to be considerably later than to
Korea, being first recorded in the Muromachi
period (1333-1568). An interest in Chinese art
had been stimulated by Zen Buddhism, which
originated in China, but it was not until the
sixteenth century that imports of Chinese blue
and white porcelain were substantial. The
shapes and spontaneous decoration of these
dishes were not at all to Chinese taste and they
were obviously made specially for the Japanese
market. The Chinese government of the time
forbade direct contact with the Japanese,
whom they regarded as pirates, so Portuguese
ships carried the porcelain to Japan.

Porcelain was not made in Japan until the
late sixteenth century. Its manufacture broke
with the tradition of Japanese ceramic production, and owed much to the influence of Korea

*Korean porcelain bottle, painted with
cobalt blue and a translucent glaze.
Sixteenth century.*

and China in its methods and decoration. Korean-style stoneware was already in production at the Karatsu kilns in northeast Kyushu.

Korean and, later, Chinese influence can be observed in the earliest Japanese porcelain, known as *shoki-imari*. Initially plain white wares were made but soon sketchy landscape and plant designs in cobalt blue were painted onto small bowls, cups, plates and bottles before they were glazed. A number of celadons and iron brown wares, as well as combinations of these colours, were also made in porcelain. The blue and white wares were similar to Chinese porcelain made during the reign of Tianqi (1621-7) towards the end of the Ming dynasty. There is some argument as to whether Japanese porcelain manufacturers were copying Chinese wares or whether the Chinese were imitating Japanese styles to compete for the domestic market in Japan.

These early Japanese porcelains were made at Izumiyama, near Arita in Hizen province in northwest Kyushu, where suitable clay had been discovered. The products of this clay, often known as Arita wares, have a thick body, as the clay was not as plastic as some of those found in China. Less plastic clay had the advantage that tall vases and jars could be thrown in one piece, whereas in China they would have been made of two or more pieces luted together. Arita ware is more opaque and greyer in colour than the translucent white porcelain produced at Jingdezhen in China. The presence of iron in the clay at Izumiyama gave the fired body a bluish tone, and the glaze, made of wood ash and clay, also had a bluish cast.

The embryonic Japanese porcelain industry expanded in the mid-seventeenth century when sources of Chinese porcelain dried up. At this time the Dutch were the only Europeans permitted to have a trading post in Japan, and the directors of the Dutch East India Company ordered their first porcelains for trade with the Southeast Asian market in the 1650s. These were mostly bottles and small pots for Javanese apothecaries in Batavia. Models were supplied in 1652 for the bottles and pots ordered for the following year. In 1657 a small chest of porcelain samples was sent to Holland and in 1659 came the first really large order for 64,866 pieces of Japanese porcelain. Much was for Mocha, Arabia, where blue and white was required, but of the 11,530 pieces destined for Holland most were enamelled.

In 1661 barber's bowls were mentioned for the first time and other European shapes such as large plates and bowls, tankards, salts and mustard pots were ordered and models sent for copying. Until recently it was believed that most of the official trade to Holland was in blue and white, but it is now known that Japanese enamelled porcelain was popular in Europe as a novelty. Chinese enamelled porcelain had not been exported to Europe in great quantity, probably because of the muddy quality of the colours on pieces available for export. The enamelled wares from Japan, on the contrary, although at first comparatively dark and opaque in colour, soon rivalled Italian maiolica.

The Dutch did not have a monopoly on the export of Japanese porcelain. The Chinese also exported it from Nagasaki and sold it on to other European companies in Guangzhou. In 1664 a Chinese junk carried 83,090 pieces of Japanese porcelain to

Pair of seventeenth-century Chinese dishes painted in the Kakiemon style.

Batavia; in the same year the Dutch shipped 68,682 pieces to Batavia. Trade with Europe continued until about 1745 after which only small amounts of Japanese porcelain were shipped to Europe.

Japanese pots were thrown on the Kyūshū kick wheel and turned, or were press moulded and turned. Cast moulds were not used until the nineteenth century. Cobalt was imported through agents in Nagasaki and painted onto the unfired body with a thick pointed brush. Glaze was applied by pouring or dipping and was a better fit than that on Chinese porcelain of the same period. The high temperature required to make porcelain was achieved in the *noborigama* kiln, consisting of a series of chambers, sometimes more than twenty, built on a hillside. There was considerable wastage, much more than the fifty per cent accepted as normal in factories today.

Porcelain for enamelling was taken to a special area of Arita, Aka-e-machi (red painting town), well established by the last quarter of the seventeenth century. Here the enamels were applied over the porcelain glaze and the vessels fired again to fuse the glass-like colours onto the clear glaze. The first use of enamels is attributed to Sakaida Kakiemon, who is supposed to have learnt the skill of overglaze enamelling from a Chinese craftsman in Nagasaki. The Kakiemon palette includes an opaque yet brilliant azure blue and a soft orange red associated with the persimmon (*kaki*) from which Kakiemon gets its name. Designs are often understated and asymmetric. The white

Imari ware bowl with polychrome enamelled design. Japan, about 1800.

porcelain space characteristic of this ware is as important as the design. The pair of dishes painted in Kakiemon style have a blue tinge in the glaze and are likely to have been made elsewhere than in Arita in imitation of this popular ware.

Imari, the port through which the porcelain for export passed on its way to Nagasaki, gave its name to enamelled ware from Arita. The Dutch were not permitted to travel to the porcelain producing areas so they identified this style of ware with the port. The

Pair of Nabeshima ware plates fired at kilns north of Arita, Japan, about 1800.

bowl decorated with ships and Dutchmen is an example of Imari ware and displays the typical multicoloured palette.

In contrast to the centralized Chinese mass production of high quality wares, Japanese porcelain was made in family kilns with a small labour force and little specialization. They had difficulty producing large numbers of identical pieces and keeping to the short delivery periods imposed by the Dutch. However, even after trade reopened with China in 1683, Japanese porcelain decorated in overglaze enamels remained popular in Europe into the middle of the eighteenth century. The Chinese made cheaper copies of both Kakiemon and Imari ware.

Both blue and white and enamelled wares were also made in Japan for the domestic market. The two plates illustrated are examples of Nabeshima ware, made at kilns north of Arita for the Nabeshima clan of feudal lords. A high standard of potting and decoration is characteristic of Nabeshima ware as it was reserved for private use. It was not known in the West until the late nineteenth century. This pair of plates was made in about 1800. The blue and white design on the outside of the plates has been sketched before being filled in with a blue wash, typical of this kiln, and the Nabeshima family crest is painted in green and red enamels over the glaze in the centre of each dish.

Figure of a wild boar made at the Mikawachi kiln, Hirado Island, Japan.

A fine quality white clay, from Amakusa Island, off Nagasaki, was used at the Mikawachi kiln, set up by potters from Hirado Island in the late seventeenth century. The best pieces were reserved for the Prince of Hirado and few came onto the open market until the nineteenth century. The Hirado potters were skilled in moulding and applied work and many pieces made from 1800 onwards were purely decorative presentation pieces, such as this boar, made around 1810.

From the late eighteenth century porcelain manufacture spread rapidly to many centres in Japan including Kyoto and Seto. Today it is made all over Japan in many styles and forms. The Kakiemon family still makes porcelain in Kakiemon style in Arita, and the skills of the Nabeshima potters continue in the Imaemon family. In Kyoto the blue and white tradition of *sometsuke* has been reinterpreted in the work of the Kondo family. Kondo Yuzo produced his first ceramics around 1910 and was made a National Living Treasure in 1977. The clear blue and white of his exquisite pieces is sometimes enhanced by red and gold. His grandson, Kondo Takahiro, is also an innovative potter. The environment in Japan today is no longer one surrounded by and in tune with nature, but manmade and artificial. Few materials are used in their natural state, so the rhythms and tensions influencing artists today are very different from those of even fifty years ago. Takahiro's work reflects these modern influences and his interest in time and space. His ceramics are often geometric, built of slabs of clay. His motifs derive from water, motion and the tensions of crowded modern life. The designs are still restrained and elegant, but the influence and impetus has changed.

Time and Space, a slab-pot in geometric form, made by Kondo Takahiro in Japan in 1995.

METAL

Ever since its initial exploitation by China's earliest known dynasty, the Shang (c1600–c1050 BC), bronze has been highly valued by the Chinese. An alloy of copper and tin, and a small amount of lead, bronze was expensive and labour intensive to produce and required a high degree of craftsmanship. As a precious material, it was quickly monopolized by the wealthy and powerful in Chinese society.

Throughout the Shang and the Zhou periods (c1600–221 BC) a wide variety of weapons and vessels were cast in bronze. These were made for the ritual offering of wine and food to the ancestors and buried with their owners in elaborate tombs as a mark of status. The ritual food vessel illustrated here is called a *gui* and would have been one of a set of vessels of different shapes for use in a ceremonial banquet. Its monster-head handles and narrow bands of stylized decoration, with an animal head on either side of the upper band, are typical of *gui* made at the end of the Shang and the beginning of the Western Zhou period, about the eleventh century BC. A single character cast into the interior of the piece signified ownership and is probably a clan name. The surface patination, caused by corrosion from damp burial conditions, became a source of admiration for later generations of collectors. This *gui* would have been made in the same way as other bronzes of the period, by means of ceramic piece moulds. A model was made, probably in clay, of the vessel to be cast, complete with incised decoration, and, when this had hardened, more clay was wrapped around it. The clay wrapping was removed by cutting it into sections and detailed decoration was added before the mould sections were fired. The mould sections were reassembled around an inner core, the two kept separate by spacers positioned at regular intervals. The whole was finally turned upside down and molten bronze poured into the space between the outer mould and the inner core. Once the bronze had set, the moulds were broken away to reveal the hollow bronze vessel. The amount of bronze required was enormous, yet a huge number of vessels have been found in tombs. That the Chinese chose to use bronze in this way, rather than simply for weapons, indicates the great value attached to the metal and to the ceremonies in which the vessels were used.

Although the use of bronze vessels in ritual diminished and the quality of the vessels declined from the Han period (206 BC–AD 220) onwards, they continued to be made, along with objects for the scholar's desk, mirrors and decorative items. This altar vase

Bronze ritual food vessel of a type used at Chinese ceremonial banquets during the eleventh century BC.

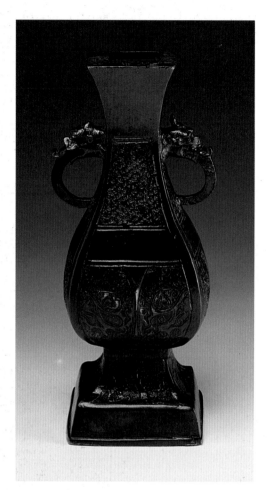

made for holding flowers dates from the twelfth to fourteenth century. It has some of the characteristics of ancient Shang and Zhou bronzes, such as the monster-head handles and the stylized decoration, but applied to a shape derived from a Han dynasty vessel called a *hu*. A hybrid vase such as this *hu* highlights the importance attached to works of antiquity and in particular to ancient Chinese bronzes. By the time of this *hu*, the method of bronze casting had changed and the lost wax process was used. A model was made in wax over a clay core which was then covered by an outer clay mould. The wax was melted out and replaced with molten metal. Once the bronze had hardened the clay moulds were broken. This is the method traditionally used in the West. Many bronze vases like this *hu* were exported to Korea and Japan from the Song dynasty (960-1279) onwards. They were used in temples, for flower arrangements in the home and as utensils in the Tea Ceremony. Many of these later bronzes entered European museum collections during the vogue for Art Nouveau in the late nineteenth and early twentieth centuries, when they came directly from Japan. They were therefore thought to be Japanese, not Chinese, in origin.

Chinese altar vase for holding flowers, made in a hybridized style between the twelfth and fourteenth centuries.

Bronze was also used in China for casting religious images. Most were portable and intended for small altars in the home. Many were gilded with a thin layer of gold leaf applied to the heated bronze surface. This figure is of the bodhisattva Avalokitesvara, known in China as Guanyin, 'he who hears the prayers of the world'. Bodhisattvas are deities who have reached nirvana or eternal paradise but who choose to return to earth to help people. This image dates to the eighteenth century, although it is Ming early fifteenth-century in style. In both the fifteenth and eighteenth centuries the influence of Tibetan Buddhism

Chinese gilt-bronze figure of the bodhisattva Guanyin made in the eighteenth century but in an early fifteenth-century form.

was particularly strong in China, and gilt-bronze images such as this were regularly exchanged between the Chinese court and Tibetan lamas. Guanyin wears elaborately flowing, rather feminine garments, a headdress containing at its centre an image of the Buddha Amitabha, of whom Guanyin is a manifestation, and sits in the position known as *maharajalilasana* (royal ease). Because of his merciful aspect Guanyin became one of the most popular Buddhist images worshipped in China. Indeed, from the Song period Guanyin was often represented as a female deity, the Goddess of Mercy, frequently in poses similar to those of the Madonna and Child in the West.

Although bronze was the most precious and most frequently used metal in China, copper, gold, silver and iron were also worked. Iron was cast into weapons, bells and images, such as this seated figure of an official, probably Wen Chang, a Tang dynasty writer later deified as the God of Literature. As most Chinese families traditionally aspired to officialdom and social and material success, many temples were dedicated to Wen Chang. The inscription on the reverse of this figure tells us that it was dedicated to such a temple, and dates it to 1491. It would originally have been covered by a layer of gesso (a plaster-like coating) and painted or lacquered, hence the rough nature of the casting. Traces of red and gold pigment can still be seen.

If ancient Chinese bronze ritual vessels represent the apotheosis of Chinese crafts-manship in metal, the weaponry of the Japanese occupies a similar position of triumph in Japanese metalwork. The Japanese sword is renowned for its quality and effectiveness. The most treasured possession of the samurai (a member of Japan's hereditary military class), the emblem of his virtue and honour, and the symbol of his way of life, the sword is venerated both in Japan and among collectors in the West. Indeed, some swords are thought to be manifestations of gods from Japan's native religion, Shintō. The making of the blade and the decoration of the sword fittings demanded the highest quality work from schools of swordsmiths and, later, metalworkers.

The earliest swords found in Japan were brought from China and Korea. Copied in Japan, they formed part of a sophisticated iron weaponry which flourished in the Kofun period, from the fourth to the sixth century AD. These early swords were single edged and straight, but by the tenth century the single-edged curved sword, so distinctively Japanese, had appeared. Blades were made of graded steel, welded and then folded back on itself. Repeated folding and hammering produced many thousands of layers of steel. Finally, before sharpening, the blade was covered in clay, which was partially removed to leave the edge of the blade free, so creating a decorative pattern known as a *hamon* when the blade was tempered. Tempering or hardening the blade was done by heating it in a pine fire and quenching it in warm water producing a hard edge with a tough resilient core that would not snap when the blade struck hard objects. Shintō rituals

Chinese iron figure, probably the God of Literature.

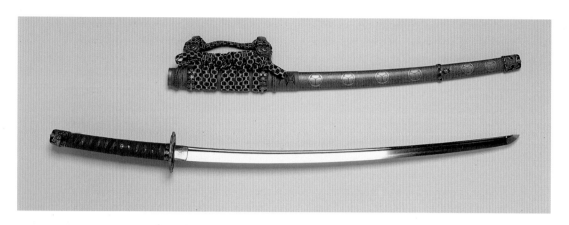

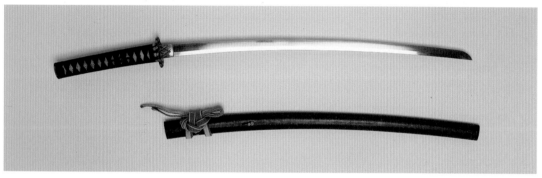

Slung sword tachi *(above) with seventeenth-century blade and nineteenth-century mounts, and long sword,* katana *(below) with fifteenth-century blade and nineteenth-century mounts.*

surrounded this technique which remained the basis of sword manufacture until the end of the nineteenth century. Swordsmiths ranked high in the artisan class, and from the Heian period (794-1185) it was common for them to carve their name, province and sometimes the date of manufacture on the tang of the blade.

Heian period blades were long and narrow from the tip to about half way down, so the sword was light and easy for a horseman to manage in one hand yet had the strength at the broader curved base for a strong two-handed cut. Swords became longer in the thirteenth century when the Japanese armies fought the attempted invasion of the Mongols under Khubilai Khan who relied on massed archers and groups of infantry with long cutting weapons.

The samurai warriors, who effectively ruled Japan from the twelfth century onwards, wore two swords: the *tachi* (slung sword), slung from the girdle, edge downwards, and the *tantō* (dirk), thrust into the girdle. In the fifteenth century the large sword was abandoned in favour of two shorter ones, known as *uchigatana* (striking swords), worn thrust into the belt with the cutting edge uppermost. The two swords most commonly worn by samurai of the Edo period (1600-1868) were the *katana* and *wakizashi*. The *tachi* and dagger were worn only with full armour on occasions such as the annual procession to the capital by the provincial lords and their samurai retinues.

Sword blades are dated and classified by their shape, the type of steel grain on the back, and the form of the *hamon* pattern on the blade. Several *hamon* patterns were used by different schools up to the sixteenth century but in the Edo period some swordsmiths experimented with more exotic *hamon* to attract the newly rich merchants who were allowed to wear a short sword.

Most swords were equipped with a variety of sword fittings or mounts, which lent themselves to elaborate decoration and became works of art in themselves. Sword guards (*tsuba*) protected the hand from slipping onto the blade and from the blade of an opponent. Made of wrought iron or steel, they were first decorated in the fifteenth century, either by piercing or with inlay of brass and copper. Hilts, scabbards and pommels were also decorated. By about 1500 the minor crafts in Japan, especially metalworking, were elevated to the status of high art, and craftsmen were proud to sign their works. The veneration of the sword increased and many different techniques were used to decorate sword fittings. Iron mounts were decorated with 'soft' metals, such as gold, silver, bronze, brass, copper and three special copper alloys which were pickled to give them their beautiful characteristic colouration. *Shakudō*, copper with a small amount of gold, has a black patina when pickled, *shibuichi*, copper with silver, produces a range of

These sword fittings illustrate the skilled detailing involved in the art of metalwork in Japan.

73

shades from olive brown to a tint like oxidized silver, *sentoku*, a variety of brass, becomes chrome yellow, and copper becomes a foxy red colour. The iron base was also treated, resulting in colours ranging from russet chestnut to violet black. Guards were also made from 'grained' iron, similar to watered or damascened steel, whereby the surface was etched, and the grain thrown into relief.

The most characteristically Japanese ground treatment, often seen on *shakudō*, is known as *nanako* (literally 'fish roe'). This is a regular formation of tiny granules each formed by a blow from a cup-headed punch guided solely by hand and eye. Introduced by the Gotō family in the sixteenth century it was used by many craftsmen over the next four hundred years.

One of the earliest decorative techniques was piercing or openwork. From this developed the moulding and carving of decorative elements, in both high and low relief. Further decorative techniques included inlay, raised inlay or incrustation, engraving and chasing. In an engraved design the metal is removed from the surface, whereas a chased design is characterized by the edges of the line being slightly raised, as the chisel has displaced the metal.

From the early seventeenth century, when the Tokugawa family moved its government to Edo (present-day Tokyo) feudal lords or *daimyō* and their retinues of samurai had to be resident in Edo for six months of the year to keep the peace. Many sword-smiths therefore moved from the provinces to the towns to meet the demand. Formal scabbards worn in Edo had to be black with mounts, in the style of the Gotō family. Their work is known as *iebori* (house carving) as the family was sponsored by the ruling house. They specialized in textured surfaces on copper alloy grounds with inlaid and overlaid decoration in gold. Subject matter was taken from Chinese legends, the Nō theatre, the Tea Ceremony and music, all intellectual pastimes of the feudal lords and the shogun. The preservation of court style led to the Gotō school becoming over formalized and unimaginative, and rich samurai and merchants sought out more ostentatious styles for informal wear. For centuries the specialized schools of sword furniture makers had been directly associated with swordsmiths and armouries serving particular fiefs and *daimyō*. In the eighteenth century, however, a group of independent studios of *machibori* (town carvers) gained in importance and popularity. The work of the *machibori* is characterized by imaginative subject matter in a wide range of coloured metals.

The proscription of wearing swords in 1876 put many skilled craftsmen out of work. They had to find other outlets for their skills in a market that no longer admired quality no matter the cost. However, the new emperor was interested in preserving traditional Japanese arts and crafts and in 1870 the government had established a department for industry, the Kobushō, part of whose responsibility was the development of arts and crafts as an export industry.

The pupils of the Gotō swordsmith Ichijo made many innovations in design and extended their work in metal to objects other than sword fittings. The *machibori* artists made toggles (netsuke) of the *kagamibuta* (mirror-plate) type consisting of a decorative disc of metalwork fitting into an ivory or wooden case. These were popular with Western visitors and collectors at the end of the nineteenth century. Even the bowls and mouthpieces of pipes, originally plain, became quite ornate at the end of the nineteenth century as the techniques of the Japanese metalworkers were applied to an ever increasing range of objects for export to the West.

At the second International Exhibition in London in 1862 the British diplomat Rutherford Alcock exhibited a large variety of Japanese objects to introduce Japanese art to the British public. Chosen by a Westerner, however, these did not reflect the best of Japanese art. In the final year of Japan's military government, 1867, over thirteen hundred objects of high quality craftsmanship were sent to the Paris Exposition, and Japan continued to send material to subsequent international exhibitions. In Vienna in 1873 the Alexandra Park Company sought to purchase the entire Japanese pavilion and its contents with the aim of rebuilding it in London, and in 1874 the Japanese government set up an export company, the Kiritsu Kōshō Kaisha, to facilitate the sale.

The then director of this Museum, Thomas Archer, was on the organizing committee of the International Exhibition at Philadelphia in 1876 and the Museum bought eleven articles from the Kiritsu Kōshō Kaisha, including the large bronze incense burner. Drawings for this burner were recently found at Ueno National Museum in Japan. Many craftsmen would have helped with such a large piece, directed by Suzuki Chokichi, the famous bronze sculptor, who signed the piece. One of his eagles perches on the lid. Bronzes of the Meiji era (1868–1912) developed as a hybrid of Japanese designs on objects suitable for Western homes. Animals were particularly popular and realistically

Bronze incense burner, purchased from the Japanese export company Kiritsu Kōshō Kaisha in 1876.

sculpted, like this pair of quails, signed Katsuyoshi. A pair of vases and an incense burner were presented in 1883 by the Meiji emperor to Sir Harry Parkes who was British Minister in Japan from 1865 to 1883 and had supported the restoration.

By the late nineteenth century, therefore, Japan was exporting a considerable quantity of metalwork to the West. It must not be forgotten, however, that the West had, centuries

Pair of quails in a naturalistic style, cast in Japan during the late nineteenth century.

One of a pair of vases presented in 1883 by the Meiji emperor to the British Minister in Japan, Sir Harry Parkes.

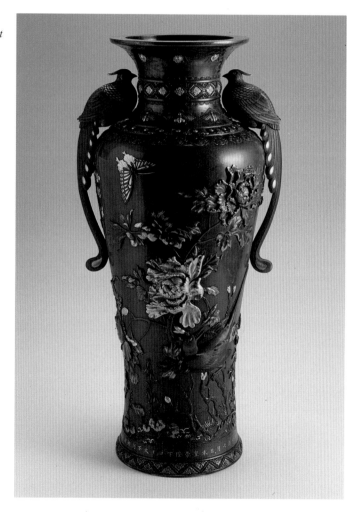

previously, been responsible for the introduction to China and Japan of two decorative metalwork techniques: cloisonné enamelling and painting in enamel. In both techniques copper or bronze served as the base. Cloisonné enamelling, possibly introduced to China as early as the Yuan period (1279-1368), but perfected in the fifteenth century, used thin strips of copper wire, cloisons, glued or soldered onto a base to make the required design. These were filled with coloured enamels and the whole fired in a low temperature kiln. There were several firings because the enamels shrank a little each time. Finally the fired enamels were rubbed down and polished until they were flush with the cloisons which would then be gilded. Many cloisonné enamels were large pieces such as incense burners made for temple or court use, but domestic pieces like this Chinese covered box were also

Incense burner presented to Sir Harry Parkes in 1883.

popular. Designed as a gift or presentation box, the decoration of a pair of mandarin ducks amidst lotus – symbols of a happy marriage – suggest that the recipient was a bride.

In Japan cloisonné enamels using gold rather than copper wires, with the translucent enamels often reflected by a gold base, were first made in the seventeenth century by the Hirata family, makers of sword furniture. The gold cloisons were set into a base of iron or soft metal. The only other type of enamelling was *champlevé*, in which the enamel is set into hollows in a metal ground, usually bronze. *Champlevé* was used to decorate small objects such as door handles and other architectural fittings in the Edo period (1600–1868). Large pieces of metalwork occasionally had small areas of enamel decoration.

Although Chinese cloisonné was imported to Japan throughout the Edo period, and the shapes were copied, cloisonné itself was not applied as sole decoration to larger

Chinese cloisonné enamel gift box, probably late seventeenth or eighteenth century, perhaps given to a bride. Enamelling as a technique was perfected in China in the fifteenth century.

Painted enamel handwarmer, made in China about 1750.

pieces in Japan until the early nineteenth century. A metalworker, Kaji Tsunekichi (1803-83) experimented with imported cloisonné from China as this was more readily available than Japanese cloisonné. By experimentation, Kaji mastered the art of Chinese cloisonné. He copied the characteristic turquoise background and made his first successful sale in 1838 to the antique dealer from whom he had bought his model. Initially his followers also made enamels in Chinese style, but Japanese motifs were soon introduced, first appearing on a turquoise background.

Early enamels consisted of a large number of wire compartments which were soldered onto a copper base. Later, techniques improved so that the gold wires became part of the design. Eventually a technique known as *musen* was developed, whereby the wires were concealed or dispensed with altogether and a gradation of colour from one area to another was possible. By 1912 Japanese cloisonné was so much in demand that factories were built to mass-produce cheap imitations. The high quality pieces produced for the world fairs and discerning customers at the end of the nineteenth century almost disappeared.

The technique of painting in enamels on copper was introduced to China by Jesuit missionaries in the late seventeenth century. In China the technique was close to that of enamels fired onto porcelain. In fact, it seems likely that painting workshops in Guangzhou (Canton) and in the Imperial Palace in Beijing, where most painted enamels were made, decorated both copper and porcelain bases. Painted enamel objects tended to be on a small scale - bowls, dishes, vases - and for personal use, such as the Museum's mid-eighteenth century handwarmer. The Chinese have always concerned themselves with warming the person rather than the entire room. Filled with hot coals this hand-warmer would have been an effective barrier against the cold.

PAPER

In AD 105, a Chinese government official, Cai Lun, submitted to the throne a method of making rag paper. It was not a new invention, as paper made from hemp and bark had been used from at least the first or second century BC, but it was a recognition by the government of the increasing use of paper as a material for writing and painting. The traditional materials were silk, which was expensive, and slips made of wood or bamboo, which were cumbersome.

It seems likely that it was the Koreans who improved the quality of paper at the beginning of the eighth century AD by inventing *tak*, a paper made from the pulp of the mulberry tree. This was of a sufficiently high quality for the printing of Buddhist texts, which constitute the largest surviving body of early prints and manuscripts on paper. Pulps from mulberry, bamboo and other plants were used to make paper in China, Japan and Korea. Bamboo produced some of the finest paper. Strips of the young plant were soaked in water, pounded and washed, and reduced to a pulp by a treatment of lime and soda. This soupy mixture was poured into a vat, a bamboo framework lowered in and a layer of pulp lifted out, pressed to release the water, and dried into sheets.

For a long time silk remained the premier material for calligraphy and painting. However, from the Song dynasty (960-1279), with the rise of the literati painting tradition whereby scholar-officials sought to differentiate their amateur, essentially intellectual, painting tradition from that of the socially inferior professional artist, paper attained an equal, if not greater, status. Prepared to receive ink and watercolours by sizing with gypsum and gum, paper was favoured by literati painters because it allowed them greater rapidity of movement with the brush than was possible on silk. The use of paper was one of the factors that encouraged the fluid strokes and spontaneity of expression that characterize Chinese calligraphy and painting.

The Museum has a fine example of literati painting on paper, an album leaf (illustrated overleaf) attributed to Wen Zhengming (1470-1559), one of the most influential literati painters of the late Ming period and founder of the Wu school of amateur painting. It is is one of a group of four which depict bamboo, orchids and grasses, executed between 1530 and 1540 after his return from government service in Beijing to his home town of Suzhou, for centuries the artistic centre of China. The subject matter of orchids behind bamboo and grasses symbolizes Wen's withdrawal from public or

The Sudden Shower on Ohashi Bridge, *one of a series of prints by the Japanese artist Utagawa Hiroshige published between 1856 and 1859.*

Album leaf attributed to Wen Zhengming, an example of literati painting on paper, executed between 1530 and 1540.

official life and reunion with close friends. He commonly used diagonal composition and the placing of the plants to one side of the picture. The sureness of Wen's technique is shown in the contrast of thrusting bamboo and elegant grasses, perfect subjects for the brush and ink technique, with the retiring orchid flower. The painting illustrates a typical feature of Chinese paintings: the application of seals. In the bottom left-hand corner are two red seals that have been applied by the artist. Both are 'fancy' or artistic names adopted by Wen and called *hao* in Chinese. Above these are two seals applied by later collectors. Chinese collectors, in a tradition alien to Europeans, would apply seals, signatures and sometimes comments to paintings in their own or their friends' collections, a convention which gave a painting an identifiable pedigree and enhanced its status if these collectors were themselves famous. The top seal is the artistic name of the early nineteenth-century monk Da Shou and the lower seal is the artistic name of Liu Shu (1759-1816), a collector in Suzhou. Both these men owned other paintings by Wen Zhengming.

Paper derived from the mulberry plant was also used for more popular prints and paintings. Mulberry paper was sized with alum before the image was applied. In the eighteenth and nineteenth centuries there was a vogue in the West for sets of watercolours illustrating every aspect of Chinese life: the manufacture of porcelain, silk and cotton, the growing and processing of tea, and botanical and topographical subjects. An example showing the processes of cotton manufacture taken from a set of about 1800 illustrating trades and occupations can be seen in the chapter on cotton (pages 92 and 96). Painted by artisans in workshops in Guangzhou (Canton), and, later, Shanghai and brought back by traders, these paintings were the postcards of their day. There is some evidence of a trade in European papers - European watermarks have been found on some sets of export watercolours.

In the mid-nineteenth century a new type of paper began to be used extensively for export watercolours. Made from the plant *Tetrapanax papyrifera, tongcao* (hollow grass) in Chinese, this thin, translucent and brittle paper was originally used for the manufacture of artificial flowers and is often referred to in the West as rice paper. Thousands of small paintings were produced on this paper in albums presenting a variety of subjects from birds and flowers to figures. The watercolour of an official playing a *qin*, or Chinese zither, is one of a set illustrating

Watercolour showing a Chinese official playing a qin, *one of a set depicting idealized Chinese subjects purchased in 1882.*

a potpourri of figures, fruits, flowers and insects in a highly detailed but purely decorative manner. The set, bought by the Museum in 1882, was probably new at the time, reflecting the tourist preoccupation with images of an idealized China.

Paper was also used in China for copying inscriptions and images from stone monuments and memorial stelae or tablets by taking a 'rubbing' or 'ink squeeze'. Copying was an accepted way of learning the art of writing and developing writing styles. Rubbings provided exact models for the student, and the activity became a respected artistic pastime with many rubbings entering Chinese collections. The method entails placing moistened paper over the area to be copied and easing it into the carved surface with a brush. A flat pad of cotton wadding covered with silk and soaked in ink is then dabbed over the paper, leaving the areas in relief black and the carved areas white.

It seems likely that rubbings of the inscriptions and images in the Wu Liang Ci, a group of offering shrines built in front of a family tomb, were taken soon after its rediscovery by Chinese scholars in the eleventh century. Constructed in AD 151 for the Wu family of Shandong province, the shrines contained stone bas reliefs illustrating good omens, the journey of the soul to heaven and the Confucian virtues of filial piety. The shrines consist of four chambers and, judging from recent reconstructions, the rubbing illustrated here comes from the west wall recess of the front chamber. It is made up of four horizontal registers, from top to bottom: a scrolling decorative band, a homage scene and two chariot processions. The stylized design of the relief sculpture closely follows that of Han dynasty paintings and sculpture and bears comparison with the earthenware tomb pillar illustrated in the chapter on pottery (pages 40 and 44).

From China paper was introduced to Japan, via Korea, about the seventh century AD. The four traditional materials used in Japanese papermaking are hemp, paper-mulberry, *gampi*, from the bark of *Wickstroemia canescens* which grows wild on the mountains and moors of Japan, and *mitsumata* (*Edgeworthia papyrifera*). Hemp was used to make the earliest paper, but most paper of the Edo period (1600-1868) is made from the paper-mulberry tree, first used in about the eighth century. Much Japanese paper is decorated, often by the random sprinkling of mica or *gofun*, a powder made from shell, onto the wet page. Together, mica and *gofun* could be added by woodblock or stencil to achieve a definite pattern. Watermarks were achieved by tying shapes of wood and metal to the drying frame so that they resisted the paper fibres and gave a patterned surface.

Although printing was probably invented in China in the sixth or seventh century, the earliest example of a printed text is Korean. Excavated in 1966 this Buddhist chant, or *dharani*, predates AD 751 when it was sealed in the Sokk-t'ap (Shakamuni stupa) at Pulguk-sa temple in Kyongju. In Japan the earliest extant printed manuscripts are the Hyakumanto *dharani*, a million of which were printed at the order of the Empress Shotoku from 764 to 770 to appease the Buddhist priesthood. It is thought that, because of the number of copies required and the even consistency, metal blocks were made for this task. The woodblock was, however, the principal vehicle for printing and would have been the preparatory stage in making metal blocks for printing the Hyakumanto *dharani*.

Before the Edo period (1600-1868) the wood most commonly used for woodblocks was the catalpa tree, although its delicate close grained quality did not facilitate clear printing. Japanese cypress was also used and by the Edo period wild cherry was popular. Blocks were cut across the grain, not parallel to it as in the West. The text, or design in the case of a colour print, was drawn in black (*sumi*) ink on a sheet of thin paper, an important stage because, although the quality of the calligraphy or design depended to an extent on the engraver, the finished woodblock reflected the quality of the original on paper. The cutting process was carried out with chisels and the design or calligraphy left in relief with the surrounding wood excised. Once the block had been washed and dried, ink was applied to it. Finally the paper was laid over the inked block and rubbed with a *baren*, a disc of twisted cord inserted into another of paper and cloth and enclosed in a bamboo sheath, which was oiled to facilitate rubbing.

From the first printed book of AD 868, Chinese books included printed illustrations, but illustrated printed books are rare in Japan until the seventeenth century, and the

Rubbing of a stone relief, taken from a Chinese tomb dated to AD 151.

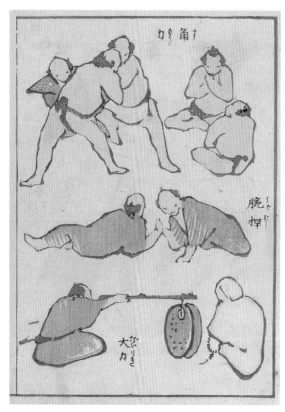

Illustrations by Japanese artist Katsushika Hokusai, active in the eighteenth and nineteenth centuries.

illustrations were applied by hand. However, there are examples of Japanese fabric printed in colour, using woodblocks, dating from as early as the eighth century. Printed colour illustrations in books did not appear in Japan until the mid-seventeenth century. In China, colour printing was developed in the twelfth century and often used for painting manuals. The albums of the Ten Bamboo Studio, 1633, and the Mustard Seed Garden painting manual, 1679, were both known in Japan.

The most common form of book binding in Japan is *fukuro-toji* (bag binding), introduced from China in the thirteenth century. Single sheets were printed on one side and folded in half so that the fold lay on the outside, making double leaves. These were sewn together at their loose edges making the spine, and the book enclosed within paper covers. The Museum's collection of about forty Japanese books, dating from the eighteenth to the early twentieth century, is mostly bound in this way.

The Museum has volumes one to thirteen of the *Manga* by Katsushika Hokusai (1760-1849). *Manga* is best translated as 'Random Sketches'. Hokusai was a prolific artist, his subjects include people in everyday life, mythological and religious figures, birds, animals, landscapes and seascapes, rivers, waterfalls, small buildings, grasses and trees. Indeed the sketchbooks contain everything a would-be artist might need as a model; it is thought that Hokusai and his publisher intended them as guides for art students. The books rapidly became popular with the public in Japan and later in the West. Another book by Hokusai, the *Ippitsu Gafu* (one brushstroke style), contains miscellaneous sketches in simplified style. The figures of sumo wrestlers and arm wrestlers are imbued with life.

Japanese fairytales were also popular in the West and the Museum has a series of these

Inside the illustration:

for was he not the son-in-law of the Sea-God, the husband of the lovely Dragon Princess?

Pages from a book of Japanese fairy tales, printed in English in the nineteenth century.

printed in English on Japanese paper and illustrated with colour prints (see also page 6). Many were translated into English by Basil Hall Chamberlain, a professor at Tokyo University at the end of the nineteenth century. He is said not only to have introduced Japan to the West but also to have taught 'Japanese and Japan to the Japanese'! Bound in small books, most of these fairytales were illustrated by Yosai Yeitaku and published by Hasekawa Takejiro between 1886 and 1892.

Japanese prints were admired by Vincent van Gogh, who is thought to have bought some in Antwerp in 1885. By 1887 he had his own collection and later made copies in oils from the series *One Hundred Views of Edo* by Utagawa Hiroshige (1797-1858). Published between 1856 and 1859 the most successful prints in this series depict the elements. The *Sudden Shower on the Ohashi Bridge* (page 80) shows pedestrians caught in

Triptych of battle preparations, by Utagawa Kuniyoshi, printed in Japan in the nineteenth century.

heavy rain seeking shelter under their umbrellas, one almost disappearing under his straw raincape. The straight, parallel lines of rain, counterbalanced by the converging lines of the Ataka shore on the horizon and the bridge in the foreground, produce a dynamic composition which enhances the power of the rain. For his oil painting, van Gogh enlarged the image using a grid, and, by working with multiple, broken brush-strokes, created an effect closer to the French Impressionist tradition than to the flat areas of colour in Hiroshige's print.

The clear colours of the Japanese print depended on a lengthy and exacting process involving a team of craftsmen led by the publisher who owned the workshop and often the sales outlets. He commissioned the artist and employed a draughtsman to transfer the design to thin translucent paper that was pasted face downwards on the block. The engraver cut at both sides of the artist's line, imitating the brushstrokes of the original drawing which was destroyed as he worked. The artist's final outline was left raised in intaglio and several proofs were taken from this key block. The colours indicated by the artist were marked up on these, each colour on a separate print so that the engraver could cut the colour blocks. A separate block was cut for each colour unless two colour areas were small and well separated in the design. A large trough was cut between the mass of colour and the rest of the uncut block to avoid overprinting.

The blocks were washed and dried and passed to the printer who mixed the colours. The inks were applied to the blocks and the paper laid on top. The quality of the paper was all important as it had to be soft enough to allow good absorption of the pigments and strong enough to withstand the printing process. As many as twenty blocks could be used for one print, each impression involving rubbing the back of the paper with the *baren*. Compositions often covered more than one sheet, as in this triptych by Utagawa Kuniyoshi (1797-1861) of large half-length figures (opposite). It illustrates the gathering of Tosa-bo Shoshun and his men before their night attack on the Horikawa Palace on 10 November 1185. Yoshitsune (on the right), his mistress Shidzuka Gozen and his loyal retainer Benkei prepare to meet them. Yoshitsune, hero of the Heike wars, was persecuted by his elder brother Yoritomo who was jealous of his popularity.

The Museum's collection of Japanese prints dates mainly to the late eighteenth and nineteenth centuries. Most are bound in albums, which has helped to preserve the fugitive colours. Prints were produced in Edo (present-day Tokyo), Kyoto and Osaka. High quality engraving and printing can be seen in an album of twenty-four portraits of actors by the Osaka artists Hirosada, Sadanobu, Kunimasa and Sadamasu, printed between 1848 and 1854. Most of the actors are shown half length. Mica dust and blind printing (where an embossed effect is achieved by applying pressure to the print with no colour on the woodblock) have been employed to enhance the quality of some of the prints. The actors

Two portraits of actors, printed at Osaka between 1848 and 1854.

Print by the Japanese artist Iwao Akiyama,
reflecting a poem by Raison, 1984.
© Iwao Akiyama/JAA, Tokyo/DACS 1996

appear in well known roles from the Kabuki theatre of the time. Ichikawa Danjūrō VII is shown here as Jiraiya holding a baby and Kataoka Ichizo as the robber Ishikawa Goemon with cherry petals falling about him.

Recently the Museum has been collecting twentieth-century Japanese prints, many in a style deliberately different from that of their predecessors. The first 'creative prints' (Sōsaku Hanga) were made at the beginning of the century; the term came into general use after the formation of the Japanese Creative Print Society in Tokyo in 1918. The society's aim was to raise the status of a print to that of a primary creative work of art, and involve artists with all the stages of making a print. Since 1970 Japanese prints have become part of the international world of art and are collected worldwide. Iwao Akiyama (1921-) has developed a deliberately rough technique of puddled black ink on handmade paper with untrimmed edges, flecked with the brown fragments from the outer bark of the mulberry tree. The effect resembles the folk prints of earlier centuries. However, sketches which accompany short verses, or *haiku*, have a sophisticated tradition. The poem above the two cats is by Raison and translates 'Both here, whiskers, cats in love'.

Paper is also used in traditional Japanese houses for sliding screens (*shōji*), in which the paper is enclosed in a lattice, for solid framed sliding doors mounted with layers of paper on both sides which are often painted (*fusuma*), and for folding screens (*byōbu*) made of layers of paper mounted over a wooden frame. Light in weight, these folding screens serve as portable room dividers, and to enclose private spaces and prevent draughts. They are also used solely as decoration. Folding screens originated in China where two- or three-fold examples are represented in tomb paintings of the Han dynasty

Japanese six-fold screen of the 1950s, with reisho *style characters at the top of each section.*

(206 BC–AD 220). They were developed in Japan to include six or eight folding panels, which made them stable yet mobile. At the top of each panel of a six-fold screen made in Japan in the 1950s a stern and imposing character has been brushed in the Chinese style known as *rishu* and in Japanese as *reisho*. This is one of the five styles of Chinese script, used mainly for titles and plaques. Since the introduction of the Chinese writing style to Japan in the seventh century, Japanese calligraphy has been influenced by Chinese styles. The characters translate from right to left: arrow, sun, fire, man, book and pleasure.

COTTON

Cotton fabric is woven from a yarn spun from the long soft strands that protect the seeds of the cotton plant. This white flossy substance is harvested after the cotton plants have shed their bloom. The varieties of cotton plant are many, and are found throughout the world, particularly in places with a warm humid climate. Cotton cloth was used by the Aztecs of Mexico in the fifteenth century and some of the best cotton grows in the Nile valley. In India cotton was known as early as the third millennium BC when it was grown in the Indus valley.

It was cotton textiles from India that played an important part in the introduction of cotton to Japan by Portuguese merchants in the sixteenth century. By the late fifteenth century traders from Portugal had established trading posts in India; they were joined by the Dutch and the English. The Europeans used Indian cotton goods as barter for spices and silk at ports further east. Soon after Indian cotton came to Japan, the Japanese produced their own coarse cotton fabric. However, as they were not able to spin such a fine cotton filament as that from India they continued to use imported yarn for the best quality fabrics.

In 1830 edicts were passed in Japan banning everyone except samurai from wearing silk, embroidery and brilliant colours. Cotton was a useful alternative. *Tōzan*, a striped cotton cloth based on imported cloth from India, became popular with artisans, merchants, lower ranking samurai and entertainers, particularly Kabuki actors who often initiated fashion trends. Striped patterns were usually made while the fabric was being woven, but designs were also created by dyeing the woven fabric in a number of different ways or by using pre-dyed yarns. Patterns could also be applied to the fabric by embroidery or quilting.

Embroidery and quilting had practical as well as decorative purposes. Cotton yarn was used in embroidery in the north of Japan to strengthen and thicken garments made of hemp. *Kōgin* is the intricate pattern of white embroidery that binds the loose weave of hemp together, making it warmer. This technique almost disappeared with the availability of cheap cotton goods in Japan at the end of the nineteenth century. However, as with many crafts it was preserved by the Mingei or craft movement of the 1930s. Cotton quilting was also decorative and functional. The dense quilting on firemen's jackets helped protect the body from fire, and futons or bed covers were quilted for warmth.

Detail from one of a group of twelve watercolours illustrating the processes of the Chinese cotton industry. Produced for the Western export market about 1800.

Starch-resist furushiki, *or Japanese carrying cloth, which may have formed part of a bride's trousseau, 1868-80.*

The Japanese excelled in the technique of resist dyeing. A paste, or resist, usually made of starch, was painted on to the undyed cotton to create a pattern. When immersed in a dye solution, the areas covered with resist remained undyed, so that, when the resist was removed, a pattern of undyed areas against a coloured ground emerged. This technique is similar to batik, where the resist used is liquid wax. The resist dyeing technique is illustrated by the carrying cloth or *furushiki*, dating from the early years of the Meiji period (1868-1912). Consisting of squares of thick cotton fabric, such cloths were often part of a bride's trousseau and exhibit the family *mon* or crest in one corner. The design usually features symbols of longevity such as the crane and the turtle, or of permanence such as the combination of pine, bamboo and plum seen here. *Tsutsugaki*, a form of resist dyeing in which a rice paste resist was applied through a cone to a freehand design drawn on the cotton, was used here. Colours were built up through several applications of resist followed by immersion in a dye bath. Areas of delicate colour were applied by brush at the beginning and protected by rice paste throughout the process. Both sides of the cloth were given the rice paste treatment to prevent dyes seeping through to previous stages. Although most *furushiki* today are printed synthetic squares traditional rice resist techniques are still used in one or two regions.

The Japanese also exploited the technique of patterning cotton by weaving with pre-dyed yarn. Known in Japan as *kasuri*, this technique is more commonly referred to by its Indonesian name *ikat*. Cotton *kasuri* became the most popular material for everyday clothes in Japan in the second half of the nineteenth century. Photographs of early twentieth-century Japan show many children dressed in *kasuri* and university students wearing a uniform including a *kasuri* kimono. It was often the preferred fabric for women's working trousers.

Kasuri cloth is rarely made by hand today, but the method is the same when the weaving is done by power loom. The pattern is drawn on graph paper to calculate which parts of the yarn are to be dyed. The bundles of yarn are then measured and bound at certain points so tightly that they will resist the colour when the yarn is immersed in the bath of indigo dye. Indigo was the most important and popular dye for traditional Japanese textiles, as it was widely available and the colour range could be used decoratively. The design emerges as the yarn is woven and the undyed yarn finds its place in the weave. *Kasuri* can be applied to both weft (transverse threads) and warp (longitudinal threads), in which case blocks of white result when the parts of the thread that resisted the dye cross. This is called double *kasuri* and is seen in the upper, chequered pattern of the example from the Museum's collections. The lower design on this late nineteenth-century piece illustrates single *kasuri* whereby only the weft or warp threads are tied to resist the indigo dye.

While cotton came to Japan via sea trade, it seems likely that it first arrived in China overland from Central Asia, as the first name for it, *baidie*, derives from one of the Turkic languages. The present name for cotton, *mianhua*, came into use after cotton cultivation and spinning were developed by the Chinese during the Song dynasty (960-1279). Before this date most raw and manufactured cotton was produced in the southern provinces or imported into China from Southeast Asia, India and Iran. From the Song dynasty most Chinese cotton was grown in the Yangzi and Yellow River basins and in the coastal province of Zhejiang, although from

Textile decorated using double and single kasuri *dyeing techniques. Kyushu, Japan, late nineteenth century.*

95

One of a group of twelve watercolours illustrating the processes of the Chinese cotton industry. Produced for the Western export market about 1800.

the fifteenth century onwards cotton was produced in most parts of China. During the eighteenth century pale yellow cotton trousers known as 'nankeens' after the city of Nanjing (Nanking), the centre of the cotton textile industry, were popular export items for the Western market.

The processing of the yarn was complex and labour intensive, as can be seen from an export watercolour in the Museum's collection, one of twelve illustrating the processes of cotton manufacture and part of a large volume documenting the making of tea, porcelain and silk as well as cotton. Sets of watercolours illustrating trades and occupations, costumes, topography and manufacturing techniques of China were popular with Western merchants in the late eighteenth and early nineteenth centuries as they provided a vivid, if idealized, souvenir of China. The Museum's set, dating from about 1800, takes the viewer from the picking of the cotton through the weaving to the transportation of the fabric to the cotton merchants. In this watercolour lengths of woven cotton are being dyed and hung out to dry.

Before the Ming dynasty (1368-1644) cotton was a luxury commodity and ordinary people used hemp for making clothes. With the spread of cotton as a cash crop, it became widely available for anything from mattresses, sails and curtains to clothing and shoes. Cotton tended to be used for the undergarments of all classes, in the form of loose trousers and long-sleeved tops for both men and women, for the outer clothing of families of moderate means, and for waistbands sewn onto the silk wraparound skirts favoured by Han Chinese women. Silk was reserved for the upper echelons of Chinese society.

Because of the relatively lowly status of cotton in China, few cotton garments have found their way into museum collections, which abound in elaborate costumes in silk. However, the Museum has cotton clothing made by some of China's many minority peoples, those living to the north of the Great Wall of China, to the west in Tibet, Qinghai and Xinjiang, and to the south in Guizhou, Guangxi and Yunnan provinces. Illustrated here is a girl's cotton jacket acquired in the area of Xining, in the northwestern province of Qinghai, close to the border with Mongolia. It may be Mongolian, but is more likely to have been worn by a member of the Tu people who inhabit Qinghai and neighbouring Gansu provinces. The style of the jacket betrays influences from the Han Chinese as well as the Mongolian and Manchu traditions. The high collar and silk embroidered peony flower are typically Han Chinese, whereas the method of side-fastening was an innovation to provide double thickness and protection from the wind. Indeed, as the Mongols were a nomadic people, the cotton for this jacket would probably have been imported from China and so follows the cut of contemporary Chinese and Manchu dress, with the addition of Mongolian embroidered designs.

Girl's cotton jacket, reflecting Han Chinese, Mongolian and Manchu influences.
Qinghai province, China, late nineteenth or early twentieth century.

STONE

Stone has never been an important building material in the Far East. It has been used for sculpture, especially in China, where it was carved into monumental statues and reliefs, usually of religious significance, often sited near tombs. The indestructible quality of stone gave it associations of endurance and immortality. Some of the most impressive Buddhist sculpture in northern China, at Yungang in Shanxi province, Longmen in Henan, and Dunhuang in Gansu, was carved directly into the rock where it could be admired and worshipped by the devout. Other large stone sculptures, such as columns and stelae, served as public monuments recording important events, texts and images. Indeed, most Chinese sculpture was created to serve a purpose and was not regarded as an art form. The majority of sculptors, or, more correctly, artisans, who worked the stone, have remained anonymous.

One such functional Chinese carving in the Museum is the Buddhist votive stele carved in limestone. Stelae like this were erected in public spaces and were usually paid for by subscriptions. Donors' names would often be carved on the monument as a record of their faith and generosity. This example dates to the Tang dynasty (AD 618-906) and shows the bodhisattva Guanyin crowned and bedecked with jewellery and flanked by attendant bodhisattvas.

One branch of stone sculpture which achieved artistic status in China, though its craftsmen were again largely anonymous, was the working of hardstones, the most famous of which is jade. The word jade derives from the Spanish term *piedra de ijada* for the stone. Meaning 'stone of the colic', it was so called as it was believed to heal the kidneys. To the Chinese the life-enhancing properties of jade have always been of supreme importance: its toughness and durability have given it associations of immortality, and its beauty represents the virtues of a just man. The Chinese name for jade is *yu*, a term which covers a variety of hardstones with the quality of jade. In simple terms there are two types of jade: nephrite and jadeite, similar in appearance but different in mineral composition. Until recently it was believed that nephrite came only from Siberia and Chinese Turkestan, but research suggests there were sources of nephrite in some of the areas of China where jadeworking developed. Until the eighteenth century, nephrite was the only kind of jade used in China. Thereafter jadeite from Burma gradually replaced it, and today most Chinese 'jade' carvings are of jadeite.

Limestone Buddhist votive stele, carved in China during the Tang dynasty.

Jade occurs in a wide variety of colours, but white and pale green are the most favoured by the Chinese. All jades are tough, compact, fine grained and take on a deep, almost translucent, lustre when polished. The toughness of jade is such that it cannot be cut or carved in a conventional manner, only abraded. To achieve this, tools like drills and toothless saws were used in conjunction with abrasive sands, like crushed quartz, mixed with water. The method remained the same until the introduction of the electrically driven lathe and diamond drill earlier this century.

Jade has always been greatly prized by the Chinese who value it more highly than gold. Even as early as the neolithic period (c7000–c1600 BC) it seems to have been used as a measure of wealth, and was buried with the deceased possibly because of its associations with immortality. The Museum has a group of small jades from burials of the Western and Eastern Zhou (c1050–221 BC) and Han (206 BC–AD 220) periods. The stylized bird pendant of the middle Western Zhou period (c900 BC) is decorated with a complex meandering pattern incised into the stone. This type of surface decoration was new in the context of jadeworking at this time. The pendant, with its small hole for attachment, may have formed part of a larger group of pendants strung together with beads and hung from the neck or waist, much like the Eastern Zhou, double-headed dragon pendant illustrated alongside it, which, although of later date (770–221 BC), was used in this way. The white bone-like appearance of the jade is thought to be the result of prolonged exposure to water, minerals, or alkaline body fluids from the deceased, during burial. Also Eastern Zhou is the sword guard. Jade sword fittings consisted of a round pommel

Group of Chinese burial jades from the Western and Eastern Zhou and Han periods.

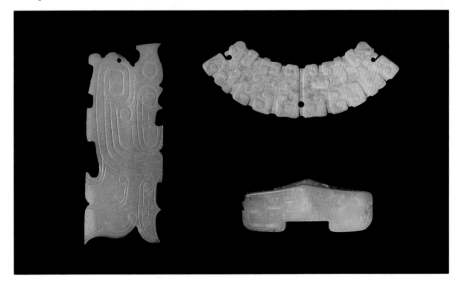

ornament, a guard, a slide for attaching the scabbard to a belt, and a protective piece for the scabbard called a chape. They became popular from about the fifth century BC when iron replaced bronze in the manufacture of weaponry and proved a less rewarding metal on which to cast fine decoration.

The disc with a hole in its centre is a *bi*. These have been found, often together with hollow jade cylinders with squared corners known as *cong*, placed around the body in burial sites from the neolithic Liangzhu culture (*c*3000 BC) to the Han. As yet, the significance of *bi* discs and *cong* is not clear, although the size and weight of some of them suggest they were not made to be worn but had a ritual use associated with burial. Early *bi* were undecorated, but, during the Eastern Zhou, surface decoration in the form of tightly curled spiral patterns was introduced, with more elaborate treatment under the Han. This *bi* disc with its relief decoration of writhing dragons probably dates from the Western Han period (206 BC-AD 9), and shows the influence of the nomadic steppe peoples of China's northern and northwestern borders. The emphasis on a strong outline and on realism is typical of designs found on bronze plaques from Inner Mongolia.

By the end of the Han dynasty in the third century AD, the use of jade in burials had declined, and there was a move to a secular use of the stone. Small carvings in the round, often in the form of real or imaginary animals, became popular as ornaments and

Bi *disc, from a Chinese burial, 206 BC-AD 9.*

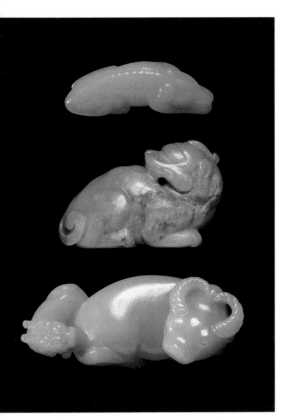

Chinese carved jade animals: naturalistic dog, 960-1279; stylized mythical beast, seventeenth century; and water buffalo with qilin, *eighteenth century.*

paperweights for the scholar's desk. It was believed that the miniature sculptures embodied the spirit of the animal depicted and great care was taken to carve the raw jade pebble in the most appropriate shape. Illustrated here are three examples from different periods. The recumbent hunting dog dating to the Song period (960-1279) is carved in a naturalistic way, while the late Ming period imaginary beast, probably a *bixie*, looking back over its shoulder, is typical of the stylized carving favoured during the seventeenth century. The depiction of a *bixie* perpetuates the tradition of the larger supernatural creatures in stone which line the 'spirit roads' leading to imperial tombs. The placement of monumental stone sculptures outside tombs coincided roughly with the decline in the number of jades buried inside tombs. The water buffalo, associated with spring and agriculture, in the Chinese folk tradition was said to have given birth to an auspicious imaginary creature called a *qilin*, seen crouching at the buffalo's tail in this eighteenth-century carving.

Other jade items included cups for wine, bowls for a variety of uses at table, and vases or containers for the scholar's desk. This eighteenth-century container for brushes in the form of a mountain landscape would have served also as an object of contemplation: a miniature world into which a scholar's imagination could retreat, symbolizing the land of the immortals as represented by the figure of the Daoist immortal Shoulao, carrying his staff and the peach of immortality.

Another desk item, an eighteenth-century brushwasher in the shape of a double gourd with a cricket perched on its side, is typical of the realism and technical virtuosity characteristic of Qing dynasty (1644-1911) carvers. This virtuosity is also seen in carvings in hardstones other than nephrite. Rock crystal, agate, rose quartz, chalcedony, carnelian and lapis lazuli were all utilized, perhaps because their appearance was different to that of jade or because they were easier to obtain and to work, and therefore less expensive. The other eighteenth-century brushwashers illustrated here are made of agate and carnelian. The agate brushwasher is carved in the form of a lotus leaf and flowers, with a frog at one end and a bird at the other. The underside of the carnelian brushwasher is carved in bold relief with a *lingzhi* fungus, emblem of longevity.

The greatest collector, patron of the arts and arbiter of taste in eighteenth-century China was the Qianlong emperor (1736-95). He was concerned with improving the quality of craftsmanship in the decorative arts, including jade carving. Qianlong composed poems to be inscribed onto prized pieces in the imperial collection. The jade tablescreen (overleaf), probably the product of the imperial court workshops, carries a poem composed by

Eighteenth-century Chinese brush holder, carved from jade in the form of a mountain landscape.

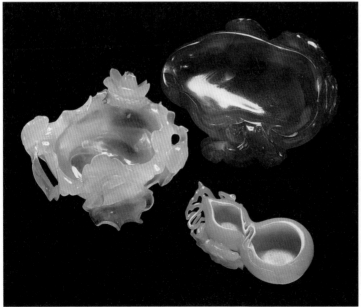

Three brushwashers of jade, carnelian and agate, made by Chinese carvers in the eighteenth century.

城南芣鄃區
野趣悦幽頂
三徑原宜句
九峯列作圖
蕭逌仙童
孝若墨後
一水平山遥
湖川烟扮行
甲辰仲春月下...

Qianlong in 1784, referring to the landscape carved on the reverse of the screen. It was once part of the imperial collection.

A stone much softer than any of the hardstones above is steatite, commonly called soapstone because of its texture. Soapstone was favoured by the scholar–gentry because its softness enabled them to carve the stone themselves and make personal seals. Commercial carving workshops also produced soapstone objects, deities and figures for the scholar's desk. This carving of a *luohan*, or disciple of Buddha, seated on a rock cleaning out his ear, was probably made at the steatite carving centre in Putian county in Fujian province during the first quarter of the eighteenth century.

Tablescreen of jade, probably carved in the Chinese court workshops. The inset shows a detail of the reverse side.

Opposite: *Soapstone figure of a Buddhist disciple made in Fujian province, China, in the early eighteenth century. Earl of Selkirk Bequest.*

IVORY AND HORN

The Chinese have been carving bone, tusk and horn since about 2000 BC. Most commonly used were elephant tusk and rhinoceros horn, but walrus ivory, whale teeth, animal bone, hornbill and antler have all been carved into vessels, figures and ornaments. Most of these materials were imported into China. Fossilized mammoth tusks were also carved.

Elephant tusks are modified teeth which grow conically from the upper part of the skull. The tip of each tusk is solid, apart from a narrow channel which carries the nerve, but the root, which is embedded in the skull, is hollow and filled with a soft pulp. The shape of the hollow root end lent itself to the carving of brushpots and other containers, and, cut into sections, it made an ideal convex wrist rest. Similarly objects made from the solid part of the tusk reflect its tapering shape. This figure of one of the eight Daoist immortals, possibly Liu Dongbin, follows the natural curve of the tusk and is typical of sixteenth and seventeenth-century carvings of immortals and other deities. The Daoist immortals were historical figures to whom supernatural powers were attributed. These devotional images from the Daoist and Buddhist pantheons and folk religions were made for home display and were often decorated with paint, lacquer and gilding. Because ivory was expensive, it was usual for a single tusk to be cut into several pieces and carved into a variety of different objects. A section of a tusk has been used to make the late seventeenth-century tray, which would have been for passing wine cups during poetry drinking games called *hangjiuling* (running wine order). The game required participants to complete rhyming couplets, which, if not satisfactory, would involve the

Late seventeenth-century tusk tray, used for passing wine cups during poetry games in China.

Opposite: Ivory figure of a Daoist immortal, carved in the sixteenth or seventeenth century in China.

Shallow dish of carved ivory made in China for the European market in the
nineteenth century.

forfeit of drinking a cup of wine. This tray, carved in the form of a phoenix holding a peony flower in its beak, both symbols of love and happy marriage, was probably made for a group of female players.

From the late sixteenth century ivory carving workshops were centred in the Chinese coastal province of Fujian. This was encouraged by a thriving export trade, especially with the Spanish Philippines, which spread to the port of Guangzhou (Canton) in Guangdong province in the eighteenth century, with the arrival of other European trading nations. Ivories made ideal souvenirs of a visit to China and throughout the nineteenth century the carvers of Guangzhou had a reputation for intricate work such as that on this tazza or shallow dish made for the European market. Each section of the dish is carved in relief on a translucent ground akin to filigree, while the stand is formed of a concentric ball carved in layers from a single piece of ivory. Each of the finely carved spheres making up the ball is separate from the next and can be rotated independently. This type of work usually appears as an independent decorative item known as a 'devilwork sphere'.

Rhinoceros horn is not, in fact, horn but a solid mass of hair which is not attached directly to the skull. When cut, stained and polished it takes on a golden brown colour. For the Chinese, the horn traditionally embodied magical properties of longevity and sexual prowess, and was also believed to detect the presence of poison. Although mentioned in Chinese texts of the Han dynasty (206 BC-AD 220), the earliest surviving objects carved from rhinoceros horn date to the Tang period (AD 618-906). These were exported to Japan where they belonged to the Japanese emperor Shomu, and were dedicated by his widow to the Todaiji Temple at Nara. They include pendants, amulets, handles and cups. Cups are the most common form of rhinoceros horn carving, as the hollow horn, when inverted, is a naturally shaped vessel. Rhinoceros horn cups were originally given to scholars successful in the civil service examinations, but by the seventeenth century, when this cup was made, they had become collectors' items. The shape and decoration of rhinoceros cups ranged from the imitation of archaic bronze vessels to more natural forms carved with landscape elements, like this cup. There was no centre for rhinoceros carving, but named carvers or workshops existed around the major artistic centre of the scholar élite, the Yangzi River delta, in the sixteenth and seventeenth centuries. In the nineteenth century Guangzhou (Canton) workshops produced most, if not all, of the massive rhinoceros horns carved in openwork which were prized in the Victorian parlours of Europe.

From China ivory was imported to Japan, mainly through Nagasaki in Kyushu, the only port where Chinese merchants were allowed to trade after 1639. The Chinese ivory workshops in Fujian province carved popular Chinese idols, which were exported to Japan. These figures were treated with affectionate humour, and it is thought that they influenced Japanese netsuke or toggles. Many early Japanese ivory netsuke represent

Wine cup of rhinoceros horn made in China in the seventeenth century.

Chinese subjects like Guanyu or Guandi, the Chinese general and god of war. However, they were not made in any numbers in Japan until the eighteenth century. Until then ivory was not a popular material for decorative arts, being used only for small items such as tea caddy lids and plectrums, and as inlay on musical instruments.

The netsuke was probably originally a purely functional piece of bamboo, root or other wood drilled with a hole to take cords. (Netsuke means 'root-attach'.) It was used to prevent personal accessories such as tobacco pouches, keys, money bags, chopstick kits, amulet cases, and seal or medicine cases (*inrō*) from slipping out from under a man's sash or *obi*. It was looped over the top of the sash, and the cord which ran from it to the *sagemono*, or 'hanging thing', was passed behind the sash, suspending the pouch or *inrō* below the sash. Japanese costume has no pockets and women carried their purses in their sleeves. The growth of commercial centres in Japan, reflecting the expansion of domestic trade in more peaceful times, supported a rising merchant class with a distinctive popular culture, the richness and diversity of which was constantly the subject of restrictive edicts. Netsuke, being unobtrusive and not of a very valuable material, were ideal for the discreet display of personal wealth and status, rivalling in workmanship the intricate sword fittings of the samurai and feudal lords.

Manjū netsuke, in the form of a dome-shaped rice cake (still eaten in Japan), were probably the most common form of shaped netsuke. As most are not decorated they are not popular with collectors. They are solid or in two halves held together by the cord. Those that are decorated are carved or etched. *Ryusa* are a form of *manjū* netsuke given flower and bird designs by cutting and perforating the ivory, bone or horn. The *kagamibuta* consists of a small bowl with a metal lid or cover. This often has a ring on its underside for attaching the cord which runs out of a hole in the bottom of the bowl. The lids are made of metal alloy decorated with inlay, engraving or relief carving. The *katabori*, or netsuke carved in the round, has been most frequently treasured and collected.

To minimize waste, in the early period ivory netsuke were carved from triangular sections of tusk often collected from places where plectrums were made for the stringed instrument known as a *shamisen*. However, master netsuke carvers used only the finest quality ivory, often from Annamese and Siamese elephant tusks, but also from boar, walrus, and hippopotamus, and occasionally narwhal. Horn was also carved, staghorn being the most popular, followed by water buffalo and rhinoceros horn.

A good netsuke must meet several criteria. It must be small enough to be easily passed between the hip and the *obi*, it must not have sharp points or edges, and it must be strong enough to support the *sagemono* by the cord which passes through it. The holes for the cord are on the side of the netsuke which fits most snugly into the body, often the back of a figure or the base of an animal. Finally, the patina caused by friction and use should add refinement to the netsuke rather than detract from its beauty.

The subjects of netsuke are as varied as the human imagination. Animals were popular, both real and supernatural, and in particular the twelve animals of the zodiac. Customers liked to order netsuke in the form of the animal of the year in which they

*Group of netsuke
illustrating a
diversity of subjects.*

Okimono, *decorative carving with a figurative subject,
typical of the art which flourished in nineteenth-century
Japan.*

were born. Fruits, shells, insects and fish of
ivory, horn and wood were very popular, as
were mythical figures and deities such as the
seven gods of good luck, legendary incidents
and folk tales, craftsmen, such as sandal and
mask makers, and storytellers, Nō actors and
dancers. All are carved in intricate detail.

Many Japanese houses have an alcove, a
tokonoma, for the display of flowers, a scroll or
an object worthy of contemplation, like a
special tea bowl. The idea that objects could
be admired for their inherent beauty or the
skill involved in making them had developed
gradually. Appreciation for purely ornamental
reasons, rather than for the aesthetic qualities
deriving from function was alien to Japan
before the influence of Western culture in the

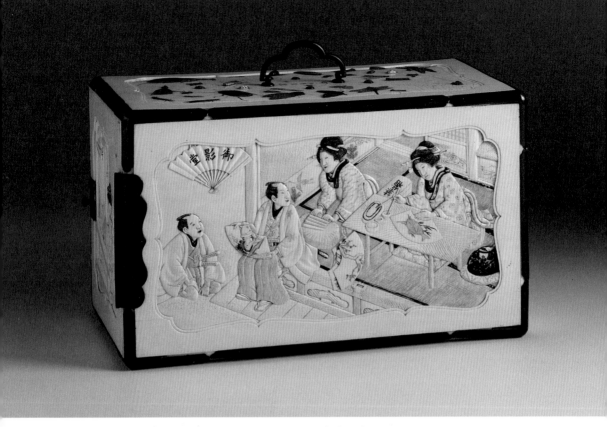

Nineteenth-century ivory Japanese box. The top is inlaid, with an insect design, in mother of pearl, horn, tortoiseshell and enamels, and the sides carved with decorative scenes.

mid-nineteenth century. After the Meiji Restoration in 1868 there was enormous demand for Japanese ornamental objects in the West, particularly those expressing the exotic lifestyle and native folklore of the East. The netsuke carvers turned to making *okimono*, or ornamental sculptures. These were larger than netsuke, without holes for the cord, and did not have to conform to a smooth rounded outline. Examples depict women dressed in kimonos with parasols, and fishermen and woodgatherers are shown with their wares on their back and often children at their feet. Samurai are carved both in armour and in court attire, sometimes illustrating legends based on Japanese history.

Ivory boxes, including tea caddies and boxes with small interior drawers, were made for foreign markets. Every available surface of the Museum's box is carved or decorated. It probably held two tea canisters, but is now empty. The scenes appear to have been picked at random for their decorative nature. A samurai on his horse in the water probably depicts an incident on the Uji River where two warriors competed to be first to cross it. On the outside of one of the doors is a weaver at her loom, and on the other are women washing clothes. Scenes are also carved on the inside of the doors. The top is

Ivory eagle, illustrating the technical virtuosity of ivory carving produced after 1887 in Japan.

inlaid with butterflies, cicadas and beetles in mother of pearl, horn, tortoiseshell and enamels.

The world exhibitions, those in Vienna in 1873, Paris in 1878 and Chicago in 1893, encouraged Japanese craftsmen to produce larger pieces. In 1887 the Tōkyō Chōkokkai (Tokyo Sculpture Association) revitalized the ivory carving industry and in the following years many large, technically dazzling pieces were produced. The ivory eagle with a wingspan of over one and a half metres, talons of horn and eyes of glass is one such piece. The head and part of the neck are carved from one piece. Many of the larger feathers are separately carved and attached invisibly to the core. The eagle used to reside in the hall of Kinloch Castle on Rhum, an island off the west coast of Scotland, where he was admired by many visitors. He came to the Museum in 1958 and, from his new perch inside the Ivy Wu Gallery, will invite visitors to embark on their journey through East Asian art.

WOOD AND BAMBOO

The paucity of good building stone in China, Japan and Korea has resulted in the traditional use of wood in architecture. Not only was wood a readily available and renewable resource, but it was also easily transported and worked. Its use as a building material is responsible for the characteristic style and construction of houses, temples and palaces throughout China, Japan and Korea.

Traditional buildings in China followed a pattern; first, a rammed earth platform, faced with stone or brick, was constructed to support a wooden framework of vertical posts and horizontal crossbeams; from these extended a complex system of wooden, U-shaped brackets which held a roof covered with ceramic tiles (page 119). External walls, which were not loadbearing, were made of wood, mud or brick; while internal divisions could be of any of these materials, they were often of wood, including elaborately carved screens and openwork panels which created a versatile space. A raised brick platform called a *kang* was used in northern China to heat the rooms, and was a seat by day and a bed at night. Portable heaters containing charcoal were used in cold weather, like the handwarmer in the chapter on metal (page 79). The drawback of wood is its vulnerability to fire, but many hardwoods had great durability and could be protected by a covering of lacquer or similar material.

Although there were regional variations in architectural style, common features were a single storey building, or for a wealthy household, several buildings, around a courtyard with a south facing entrance. This presented blank walls to the outside world, and gave the family privacy and security. The layout allowed for expansion with the addition of more buildings facing onto further courtyards. For the rich a garden might be developed in an enclosed space: a carefully contrived miniature landscape. Because of the flexibility of the traditional Chinese home, many wealthy families lived in the same residence for generations. Inside there was strict segregation: men lived apart from women, children from parents, and servants from family.

There was a variety of furniture: tables, chairs, cabinets and beds, made of bamboo and a number of different woods, which include a sought-after hardwood called *huali*, imported from Southeast Asia and renowned for its subtle colour and beautiful grain. *Huali* ranges in colour from a pale yellow to a purplish red, and is the wood used to make the square table in the Museum's collection, which dates to about 1600. It displays the

Temple guardian, one of four heavenly kings that protected a Buddhist temple. China, seventeenth century.

sophistication of design and construction typical of cabinetmakers of the late Ming period, and has a typical mitred, mortice and tenon frame with floating central panel, and recessed legs joined by a humpbacked stretcher and apron. No screws or nails were used. It would have been used for a variety of purposes from writing to dining and, like other pieces of furniture, placed against the wall when not in use. Furniture was made throughout China, but two of the main centres of production were Suzhou and Guangzhou (Canton).

Wood was also used for carving. Sculptures ranged in size from small desk objects to large figures for temples. Illustrated here is a seventeenth-century figure of one of the Four Heavenly Kings (*si da tian wang*), one of a pair in the Museum's collection but, as the title suggests, originally one of four (page 114). Placed in pairs on either side of the outer entrance of a Buddhist temple, such armoured figures served as guardians or protectors of the four quarters: North, South, East and West. Both figures in the collection are covered with a ground of gesso (a plaster-like substance), and painted with layers of red and black lacquer, silver and gilding, applied at various times in the

Table of huali *wood, carved about 1600 in Suzhou or Guangzhou, China.*

sculptures' history. This is probably Zeng Zhang (increased grandeur), King of the South, whose colour is usually red. His attribute (now missing) is normally an umbrella, which, when raised, induces violent thunderstorms, or perhaps it represents Guang Mu (Large Eyes), who presides over the West and carries a sword in his left hand. The other figure in the collection is that of Duo Wen (one who hears everything), King of the North. Called the Black Warrior, his emblem is a jewel, which he holds in a seal-shaped box in his right hand. It is likely that the design source for temple and domestic shrine figures was woodblock prints and illustrated books. Their lively linear images translated successfully into this type of carving.

Chinese carvers also worked materials which are not strictly woods at all: coconut shells, dried gourds, fruit stones and, most importantly, bamboo. The bamboo (*Bambusa arundinacea*) is a grass characterized by tall, jointed, hollow stems or culms segmented by knotty joints or nodes. Bamboos grow in most parts of China, especially well in the southern provinces. There are more than one thousand species of bamboo, some growing to a height of 15 metres, with a diameter of up to one metre. The most popular species for carving is *maozhu (Phyllostachys pubescens)* grown in the southeastern province of Zhejiang. Both the stem and the root lend themselves to carving.

Before bamboo is carved it is boiled and left to dry out for several years. Depending on the effect required, the skin is either left on or scraped off. The hollow stems of bamboo make ideal brushpots, perfume holders and other cylindrical receptacles and, cut longitudinally, the slightly curved oblong strips serve as wrist-rests for use when writing with a brush. This brushpot is carved in openwork with a design of Laozi, the reputed founder of Daoism, who

Brushpot carved from a length of bamboo. China, eighteenth century.

Eighteenth-century figure of Shoulao, the God of Longevity, carved in China from a bamboo root.

rode westward on a buffalo and was seen no more. The landscape of pines and prunus, together with the bamboo of the pot itself, symbolizes longevity and the qualities of the perfect gentleman - steadfastness and resilience. Indeed the association of bamboo with the gentleman was probably one of the reasons why it became a popular material among the scholar-gentry, many of whom carved it themselves. Stripped of its skin, this brushpot has been polished to a wonderful lustre. As with temple figures, the source of the design was probably a woodblock illustration. The twisted irregular shape of the bamboo root provided endless inspiration for the craftsman. This small figure of Shoulao, the God of Longevity, with his peach of immortality, is carved from a bamboo root with the skin retained. This technique is called *zhu huang* (bamboo yellow) in Chinese and it allows the delicate pale skin to create a very subtle speckled effect. Both these bamboos were carved in the eighteenth century when bamboo carving was reaching the end of the success it had enjoyed since the sixteenth century.

A number of bamboos bear the signatures of their carvers, some of whom were well known scholars. However, most were made by anonymous craftsmen in commercial workshops, the best known centres of production being Jiading in Jiangsu province, base of the Jiading school, and the city of Nanjing, where the Jinling school worked. Bamboo carvers in the Jiading tradition were renowned for deep sculptured effects, while the Jinling school was noted for shallow carving. It seems likely that the Museum's brushpot (page 117) was made at Jiading.

The majority of early Chinese Buddhist architecture has been destroyed. But the spread of Buddhism from China to Japan, partly through Korea, from the sixth century AD, resulted in the transmission of many elements of Chinese Buddhist architecture to Korea and Japan. The earliest extant wooden Buddhist temple is in Japan, near Nara: the Hōryūji, built as a private temple for the crown prince Shōtoku in the seventh century. The main hall of worship, the Kondo (Golden Hall), is constructed in the Chinese style. In the ninth century a new rigorous sect of Buddhism arose in opposition to the wealthy and powerful sect centred in the capital, Kyoto. Led by Kūkai, who had studied esoteric Buddhism in China and is known posthumously as Kōbō Daishi, the sect built temples away from Kyoto in the surrounding hills. The most characteristic temple of this style is the Murōji, set amongst cypress trees on the hills to the southeast of Nara. Cypress bark is used for the shingled roof, instead of ceramic tiles, and more wood is used in the structure of the building than in China or Korea, with wooden planks replacing the earthen floors of earlier Buddhist architecture in Japan.

Hōryūji temple colonnade. Japan.

Detail of a traditional Chinese roof.

Cedars line the way to the main shrine at Ise, Japan.

Japan was fortunate to have enormous resources of cypress and cedar, both excellent building woods. Korea, on the other hand, has granite uplands and shale regions in the south-western plains, neither of which is suitable for good forestry, although pine and fir trees are grown. The most widely used wood is pine (*Pinus densiflora*) but, as it is hard to work with, pillars supporting the wooden crossbeams for the rafters and tiled roof are often of stone. Roofs are hipped or gabled, or both. Earthen walls are built between the pillars and the cross-beam on a wooden grid strengthened by bamboo splits. These walls are finished on the exterior with plaster and papered inside. Small storm windows are framed into the walls for ventilation rather than for letting in sunlight, as, in general, Korean houses are built to keep out the severe winters.

Inner latticed doors are papered on one side only to allow light to filter into the rooms. Many of the designs created by the wooden door ribs are based on interlocking grids with rectangles of several sizes. Some designs cover the whole door whilst others are placed at the edges and centre to leave much of the space uncluttered.

Korean houses are usually smaller and lower than those of the Japanese, and have an under-floor heating system (*ondol*). Stone plates, which retain the heat from below, are spread with a mud floor, often covered with oiled paper or wood laid in designs. Korean furniture is generally of wood, and much of it is low so users could take advantage of the heated floor. Low tables made it possible to sit on cushions on the floor, or on low seating with separate armrests. Wooden beds were low, for warmth, and some had storage space below a slatted platform. The exception to this low furniture is the wardrobe, which consists of tall, square, free-standing display shelves with integral cupboards and storage chests often arranged in vertical pairs, one on top of the other. It is used for clothes and blankets.

The traditional Korean home was divided into male and female apartments. The master of the house had a study and drawing room where guests were received. Typical furniture included reading and writing tables, document chests and cupboards with several display shelves above them. In the women's quarters the business of running the household took place. Much of the furniture was made up of chests arranged vertically in matching pairs, or even three pieces one on top of the other. Female guests were entertained in these rooms, which often had beautifully crafted wooden toilet boxes with fold-away mirrors and sewing boxes, and folding screens, painted with birds and flowers.

Chests were used for the storage of clothes, usually folded rather than hung, and bedding. The type of chest known as *bandaji* is rectangular, with the upper half of the front hinged at the base and opening downwards. If it was to be used for storing books or scrolls it had small drawers and cupboards inside and was kept in the male quarters. *Bandaji* with no interior fitments were used for clothes and bedding in the female quarters, as was the Museum's mid-nineteenth-century example. It is made of zelkova, a hardwood of the elm family, and its fine colour and grain are exploited to the full. The

Wooden chest for storing clothes and bedding in the female quarters of a traditional Korean home in the nineteenth century.

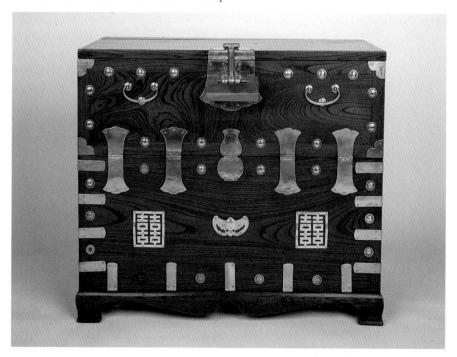

brass fitments on chests often expressed good luck, long life and happiness, particularly as the chests were commonly wedding gifts or part of a dowry. Hinges at the base of the upper half of the chest are shaped as two spools, representing longevity, and at the centre is a hinge in the shape of a medicine bottle for good health. The characters in the lower half stand for double happiness, and the bat is a symbol of good luck. The brass bosses are said to represent the big dipper, another symbol of longevity. The chest is made of planks of wood joined at top and sides with finger jointing. The brass hinges and splice plates strengthen the joins and add to the distinctive style of the chest, placing its manufacture in the Kyoung-gi-do area around Seoul.

As with traditional Chinese and Korean buildings, the structure of a Japanese house relies on a wooden frame placed on stone supports. A shingled, thatched or tiled roof has overhanging eaves to provide shade from the direct heat of the sun. In winter the low sun warms the rooms on sunny days, but bad weather can be shut out by a series of screens. Inside, a series of rooms opens onto each other, some enclosing inner courtyards. The whole is surrounded by a veranda which acts both as a passageway between the rooms and as transitional space between interior and garden. Sliding wooden storm shutters (*amado*) on the outside of the veranda can be closed in bad weather and at night, but slide open during the day to allow air to circulate, essential in Japan's humid climate. The inner rooms are partitioned with sliding screens, to increase the flow of air and the flexibility of the space. Sliding screens (*shōji*), described in the chapter on paper, allow the light to pass through.

Japanese rooms tend to be sparsely furnished, particularly reception rooms in the castles of the military classes of Japan, where decoration consisted mainly of bold, colourful designs painted on screens. Furniture included low writing tables and matching writing boxes made of lacquered wood sprinkled with gold, black lacquer covered tables and trays, and display shelves with integral cupboards.

In the tea house wood was not lacquered but left untreated to increase the rustic harmony (*wabi*) central to the Tea Ceremony. Japanese cypress was used in its natural state in the main building dedicated to Amaterasu, Goddess of the Sun and ancestor to the imperial line. It has a delightful fragrance and subdued lustre, prized for temples and shrines and for Buddhist sculptures.

Wooden Buddhist sculpture was made in Japan from the sixth century, and until the ninth century there was a preference for unpainted images. However, pigmented or gilt wood later became the norm for temple images, so they stood out against the dark interiors of Buddhist temples. The images were covered in white gesso, then lacquered and painted in bright colours and gold. Enkū (1628-95), a Buddhist priest and famous sculptor, carved wooden images which he left at shrines as he travelled the length and breadth of Japan. Chisel marks remain in the wood and the rough vague features evoke a sense of mystery and power alien to more conventional sculpture.

The small sculptures called netsuke were discussed in the chapter on ivory and horn. They were also made of wood, the most suitable being boxwood. Its strength supports

Group of netsuke, carved in Japan from a variety of woods in the nineteenth century.

a tobacco pouch, medicine case or personal seal, and its fine, even grain produces a lustrous patina that improves with use and age. Boxwood from Mount Asakuma, near Ise, is the best for carving and was used by netsuke carvers in Nagoya and Ise. The monkey and the rat are zodiac animals which were a popular subject with netsuke artists. Ebony and cherry were frequently carved, as were zelkova, camphor, pine, camellia, bamboo and yew. Nuts, peach stones and fragrant wood such as sandalwood made unusual netsuke. Some wooden netsuke are painted or lacquered but most are simply carved, exploiting the natural beauty of the material.

Sets of wooden shelves, usually with lacquer decoration, had been made in Japan for the domestic market since the eleventh century. The setting of cupboards into these low shelves was a common design feature. The edges of the shelves and of the overlapping top rise up in imitation of the paperweights found at the ends of traditional writing tables. Pairs of such shelves were made as part of a bride's dowry furniture and were used to display objects from her dowry. They had an open shelf under the top, and cupboards

Cabinet with drawers, probably made for the Western market in the late nineteenth century, perhaps to hold curiosities.

placed diagonally across from each other on the two lower shelves. Many bear the *mon* or family crest. The cabinet on display in the Museum is narrower and taller than traditional Japanese shelves and includes a stand, not typical of its forerunners. The inclusion of drawers, a Western innovation, suggests the cabinet was probably made for the Western market at the end of the nineteenth century. The decoration exhibits a variety of wood veneers including oak, coromandel, elm, and fruit woods, particularly pearwood, kingwood and satinwood, often used in marquetry. Lacquered panels decorate the drawers in the sliding cupboard at the top, and the centre panels of the cupboard at the bottom. This cabinet may have displayed curiosities from foreign lands in a Victorian drawing room of the 1860s. It illustrates the way in which objects from the East were first collected in the West for their exotic and strange nature and then placed out of context in a culture which understood neither the techniques of their manufacture nor their original function.

The Japanese cabinet provides a fitting conclusion to this brief survey of the materials used by the peoples of China, Japan and Korea. Not only does the cabinet appear exotic, as did so many of the items seen by Marco Polo during his travels in the east in the thirteenth century, but it also epitomizes those luxuries that were imported to the West and used for purposes quite different from those for which they were originally intended in the East. In the Museum, however, this cabinet can be appreciated by a large audience who, thanks to modern scholarship, have the chance to gain some understanding of its manufacture and original function.

FURTHER READING

CHINA

BLUNDEN, C and M Elvin. *Cultural Atlas of China.* Oxford, 1983.

BRINKER, H and A Lutz. *Chinese Cloisonné: The Pierre Uldry Collection.* New York and London, 1989.

CLUNAS, C (ed). *Chinese Export Art and Design.* London: Victoria and Albert Museum, 1987.

CLUNAS, C. *Chinese Export Watercolours.* London: Victoria and Albert Museum, 1984.

DICKINSON, G and L Wrigglesworth. *Imperial Wardrobe.* London, 1990.

HU SHIH-CHANG. *2000 Years of Chinese Lacquer.* Hong Kong, 1993.

KERR, R. *Later Chinese Bronzes.* London: Victoria and Albert Museum, 1990.

KERR, R et al. *Chinese Art and Design; The T T Tsui Gallery.* London: Victoria and Albert Museum, 1991.

LINDQVIST, C. *China: Empire of the written symbol.* London, 1991.

RAWSON, J. *Ancient China; Art and Archaeology.* London: British Museum, 1980.

RAWSON, J. *Chinese Ornament: The Lotus and the Dragon.* London: British Museum, 1984.

RAWSON, J. *Chinese Jade from the Neolithic to the Qing.* London: British Museum, 1995.

RAWSON, J (ed). *The British Museum Book of Chinese Art.* London: British Museum, 1992.

TSANG, G and H Moss. *Art from the Scholar's Studio.* Hong Kong, 1982.

VAINKER, S. *Chinese Pottery and Porcelain: From Prehistory to the Present.* London: British Museum, 1991.

WATSON, W. *Art of Dynastic China.* London, 1981.

WATSON, W (ed). *Chinese Ivories from the Shang to the Qing.* London, 1984.

WATT, J C Y and B Brennan-Ford. *East Asian Lacquer: The Florence and Herbert Irving Collection.* New York, 1991.

WILSON, V. *Chinese Dress.* London: Victoria and Albert Museum, 1986.

JAPAN

AYERS, J, O Impey and J V G Mallet. *Porcelain for Palaces: The fashion for Japan in Europe 1650-1750.* London, 1990.

CLARK, T. *Ukiyo-e Paintings in the British Museum.* London: British Museum, 1992.

HARRIS, V. *Japanese Imperial Craftsmen: Meiji Art from the Khalili Collection.* London: British Museum, 1994.

IMPEY, O. *Dragon King of the Sea: Japanese Decorative Art of the Meiji Period from the John R Young Collection.* Oxford: Ashmolean Museum, 1991.

JAHSS, M and B. *Inro and other miniature forms of Japanese Lacquer Art.*London, 1971.

LANE, R. *Images from the Floating World: The Japanese Print.* Oxford, 1978.

ROBINSON, B W. *The Arts of the Japanese Sword.* London, 1961.

SEIROKU NOMA. *The Arts of Japan; Ancient and Medieval* Vol 1 and *Late Medieval to Modern* Vol 2. Tokyo 1966.

SMITH, L, V HARRIS and T CLARK. *Japanese Art; Masterpieces in the British Museum.* London: British Museum, 1990.

YAMADA, CHISABUROH F. *Dialogue in Art: Japan and the West.* London, 1976

BARBICAN ART GALLERY. *Japan and Britain: An Aesthetic Dialogue 1850-1930.* London, 1991.

NATIONAL MUSEUMS OF SCOTLAND. *Behind Golden Screens: Treasures from the Tokyo Fuji Art Museum.* Edinburgh, 1991.

ROYAL ACADEMY OF ARTS. *The Great Japan Exhibition: Art of the Edo Period 1600-1868.* London, 1981.

VICTORIA AND ALBERT MUSEUM. *Japanese Art and Design; The Toshiba Gallery.* London, 1986.

KOREA

GOMPERTZ, G ST G M. *Korean Celadon and Other Wares of the Koryo Period.* London, 1963.

GORO AKABOSHI AND HEIICHIRO NAKAMARU. *Five Centuries of Korean Ceramics: Pottery and Porcelain of the Yi Dynasty.* New York, Tokyo and Kyoto, 1975.

LEE KYONG-HEE. *Korean Culture: Legacies and Lore.* Seoul, 1993.

McKILLOP, B. *Korean Art and Design: The Samsung Gallery of Korean Art.* London: Victoria and Albert Museum, 1992.

WHITFIELD, R et al. *Treasures from Korea: Art through 5000 years.* London: British Museum, 1984.

CHRONOLOGIES

CHINA

NEOLITHIC CULTURES   *c*7000–*c*1600 BC

EARLY DYNASTIES
Shang   *c*1600–*c*1050 BC
Western Zhou   *c*1050–771 BC
Eastern Zhou   770–221 BC

IMPERIAL CHINA
Qin   221–206 BC
Han   206 BC–AD 220
  Western Han   206 BC–AD 9
  Xin   AD 9–25
  Eastern Han   AD 25–220
Three Kingdoms   221–280
Southern dynasties   265–589
Northern dynasties   386–581
Sui   589–618
Tang   618–906
Liao   907–1125
Five Dynasties   907–960
Song   960–1279
Yuan   1279–1368
Ming   1368–1644
Qing   1644–1911

REPUBLICAN CHINA
Republic   1912–49
People's Republic   1949–

JAPAN
Jōmon period   *c*10,000–*c*300 BC
Yayoi period   *c*300 BC–*c*AD 300
Kofun period   *c*300–mid sixth century
Asuka period   mid sixth century–AD 710

Nara period	710-794
Heian period	794-1185
Kamakura period	1185-1333
Muromachi period	1333-1568
Momoyama period	1568-1600
Edo period	1600-1868
Modern period	1868-
Meiji era	1868-1912
Taishō era	1912-26
Shōwa era	1926-89
Heisei era	1989-

KOREA

Neolithic	c4000-1000 BC
Bronze Age	c900-400 BC
Iron Age	400-200 BC

DIVISION BETWEEN NORTH AND SOUTH

Chinese commanderies	108 BC-AD 313
Three Han states	0-AD 200

THREE KINGDOMS

Koguryo	37 BC-AD 668
Paekche	18 BC-AD 663
Early Silla	57 BC-AD 668

United Silla	668-935
Koryo	935-1392
Choson	1392-1910
Japanese colonial	1910-1945